The Researcher's Guide to Influencing Policy

Designed to help navigate the complex and ethical challenges of working with policy, this must-read book will help researchers effect changes with meaningful and widespread impact. Readers will learn how to negotiate complex power dynamics, use informing and influencing strategies and play critical roles in policy networks to give voice to those who are rarely heard in the corridors of power.

This guide is based on two decades of Professor Reed's peer-reviewed work on the impact of research and his experience using his environmental research to influence policy around the world. It covers the tried and tested practical skills needed to co-produce policy options, based on rigorous evidence and the perspectives of those whose lives will ultimately be affected by policy. Importantly, it provides the tools required to communicate research effectively to policy audiences and collect evidence of policy impacts.

Applicable to all disciplines and career stages, *The Researcher's Guide to Influencing Policy* provides the confidence needed to start engaging with policy safely, responsibly and effectively. It is time to get out of the echo chamber of research and policy elites and to start getting our hands dirty with the messy reality of real-world policy.

Mark S. Reed is Professor of Rural Entrepreneurship and Director of the Natural Capital Challenge Centre at Scotland's Rural College (SRUC), UK. He is also CEO of Fast Track Impact, Research Lead for the International Union for the Conservation of Nature's UK Peatland Programme and Co-Chair of the United Nations Environment Programme Global Peatlands Initiative Research Working Group and plays advisory roles for various UK government bodies.

The Researcher's Guide to Influencing Policy

Mark S. Reed

LONDON AND NEW YORK

Designed cover image: Cover image designed by Anna
Sutherland

First published 2025
by Routledge
4 Park Square, Milton Park, Abingdon, Oxon OX14 4RN

and by Routledge
605 Third Avenue, New York, NY 10158

*Routledge is an imprint of the Taylor & Francis Group, an
informa business*

British Library Cataloguing-in-Publication Data
A catalogue record for this book is available from the British
Library

ISBN: 978-1-032-79998-8 (hbk)
ISBN: 978-1-032-79999-5 (pbk)
ISBN: 978-1-003-49494-2 (ebk)

DOI: 10.4324/9781003494942

Typeset in Interstate
by KnowledgeWorks Global Ltd.

Contents

Acknowledgements

This book builds on a shorter handbook co-authored with Paul Cairney. Thank you Paul for your work which above all others has inspired me to think more critically about how I engage with policy, any of your text that has made it through to this book and your willingness to let me build on our joint work as a sole authored book. The original handbook was funded by the University of Leeds via Research England's QR Strategic Priorities Fund as part of Policy Leeds training provision. Thanks to Juliet Jopson and Ged Hall for constructive feedback on that work. The full book you are reading now has benefited from constructive feedback from two reviewers, Eric Jensen and Vicky Ward, and Sarah Hyde as Editor.

Thanks to the co-authors of the 3i analysis paper, particularly Eric Jensen who helped shape Table 5.2. Thanks to Laurie Prange for the firm but compassionate tweet and Josie Valadez Fraire for the poem that helped me realise the importance of questioning my use of the word 'stakeholder' and the need to try and decolonise this book. Finally, thanks to all the researchers who have attended my Influencing Policy training over the years, whose questions and ideas have helped shape much of the thinking in this book.

Courses can be booked at: https://www.fasttrackimpact.com/training-courses.

For more free resources on influencing policy, including videos and podcast episodes, visit: https://www.fasttrackimpact.com/i-want-to-influence-policy.

Sign up for my monthly newsletter at: https://www.fasttrackimpact.com/newsletter.

CHAPTER 1

Introduction

By contributing to policy, it is possible to use your research to effect change that is both deep and wide. Whether you seek to inform the policies of an organisation, local government, national policy or guidelines or influence policy on the international stage, this book will provide practical guidance on using your research to change how things are done, for the better. You will be able to identify new ways you can work with policy, whether you are a postgraduate researcher, a member of research staff or an early career or senior academic. There are strategies that will work if you are on a shoestring budget or part of a large, well-funded project. You will learn how to negotiate complex power dynamics and see how your own values and privilege influence how you act. You will learn informing and influencing strategies and explore the different roles you can play in policy networks. You will learn practical skills to communicate your research effectively to policy audiences and collect evidence of policy impacts. However, you will also be invited to question the very basis of your ability to influence policy as a member of the academic elite, influencing policy elites without reference to the people who will ultimately be impacted by the policies you shape. This is deep work, interrogating the assumption that 'evidence-based' policy is either possible or desirable, questioning why you do the research you do and asking how you can use your power to give voice to those who are rarely heard in the corridors of power. You will begin to question much of what you believe about the reality of working with policy. But you will also gain the tools you need to manage your privilege and navigate the messiness of real policy work.

To do this, I have drawn on over 20 years of experience researching and doing policy work. In researching this book, I have realised that there are many theories and strategies that might have been useful to know about years ago. But like you, I was too busy trying to make a difference

DOI: 10.4324/9781003494942-1

between the teaching and research pressures of academic life. For this reason, I wanted to write a book that you would want to make time for, that is as full of evidence as it is full of stories from someone who has experienced the same pressures and challenges as you.

If you are wondering how your research could make a difference but have no idea where to start, then I have stood in your shoes. As a young researcher, I followed my missionary ancestors to Africa, hoping like them to use my privilege to do good but having no idea how. My PhD research in the Kalahari Desert had the potential to challenge policies that were enclosing communal rangelands for use by rich cattle ranchers. Climate change was already making life hard in the villages, and these people could not afford to lose their grazing lands. I wanted to help. But my research went against the advice of government researchers and I was an outsider, trying to influence policy officials who often had their own cattle ranches. I didn't give up, eventually helping bring together two United Nations (UN) conventions to focus on the impact of climate change on deserts around the world, with the help of fellow PhD student at the time (now Professor) Lindsay Stringer. Impressive though this may sound, I often question the value of policy impacts like that, as I wonder how people in those villages, like my guide and interpreter, Alfred Chiroze, and his daughter Pearl, are making their way through a world that is even harsher now than it was when I left them. The last time I presented my research at a UN climate summit, I felt physically sick when I realised how proud it had made me feel, standing up there in front of all those important people. How many of our attempts to do good are actually, deep down, just attempts to feel good about ourselves? Even if we think we made a difference, how do we know the policies we influenced actually worked and didn't cause more harm than good? What if we are using our power as researchers to gain privileged access to people who should really be listening to the lived experiences of people like Alfred and Pearl? Is influencing policy just a process of one elite (academics) helping another elite (those who make policy), without reference to the people that the policies are meant to ultimately benefit?

Most of the toolkits and guides on how to achieve 'policy impacts' from research will tell you how to do all the things I have been doing, most of my career, as I have constantly striven to do better than the failed impacts of my PhD research. And they will make you sick. Moreover, they will contribute towards a sickness that is increasingly baked into academic life: the pursuit of impact to serve the demands of funders and governments who need to justify their investment in research. In this book, I want to propose a different path. As a busy researcher myself, I will share methods for efficiently and effectively targeting the limited time you have to get as many public benefits as possible from your work. But I will also invite you to do the deeper, more time-consuming work of interrogating how you view knowledge and evidence and how you can use your power to legitimise and give voice to those who are rarely heard. I want you to question the assumptions you make in your own research as much as you question the motives and biases of those you interact with in policy networks. In so doing, you will be able to reflect on responsible approaches to engaging with policy. You will be able to question how policy problems are framed, what solutions might be on or off the table and enable more equitable and effective policies to be developed.

WHY ENGAGE WITH POLICY?

When I speak of policy, I am talking about actions that are proposed or adopted by organisations to achieve a goal, whether they be a local charity, a national government or an international body (more on exactly what policy is and how it works in Chapter 2). But why engage with policy?

Like me, you might want your research to make a difference. Alternatively, you might be more driven by curiosity, seeking to identify new, challenging research questions that might advance the cutting edge of your discipline as much as it might benefit policy. By engaging with policy, you might find yourself intellectually stretched more than ever before, as you encounter challenges that do not respect disciplinary boundaries. This in turn may encourage you to engage with new people from research, policy and practice, who might challenge your assumptions and extend your thinking in creative new ways.

It is important to understand how engaging with policy might relate to your intrinsic motivations as a researcher rather than just being driven by extrinsic incentives. I once mentored a colleague who told me they had chosen me as their mentor because having a highly scored impact case study in the UK's Research Excellence Framework was one of the criteria for promotion to Senior Lecturer. While it is great that universities are rewarding researchers for engaging with impact, if this is your main motivation for doing good, then if not declared, this could undermine trust in you as a researcher. If not disclosed, the fact that you might get promoted or your institution could receive large sums of money could undermine trust in you and other researchers. I would also question whether you will be in this for the long haul; if it turns out that the people you are helping won't be able to give you the evidence of impact you need, in the right timeframe, will you continue helping them simply because it is the right thing to do?

Ultimately, there is nothing wrong with integrating policy impact into proposals or writing your impact up as a case study, but to make it more sustainable, you have to find your own reasons for investing your time and energy in policy work. Whether it's the thrill of knowing you made a difference, the curiosity or challenge of answering complex policy questions in the real world or you just want to meet and work with interesting new people, do this work because you really want to, not because someone else wants you to.

WHY DO POLICY COLLEAGUES WANT TO WORK WITH US?

Whether or not you want to work with people in policy, people in policy may want to work with you. Evidence analysts in government bodies are looking for high-quality, impartial and accessible information to solve problems, brief strategy teams and ministers and develop new policies. Parliamentarians may be looking for evidence to support or oppose the introduction of new legislation or inform debate. A 2015 survey of over 2000 Australian policy officials by Joshua Newman and colleagues, published in *Public Administration Review*, suggested that more than 60% used academic research in policy reports. A similar survey of UK politicians and parliamentary staff found that 98% found research useful in their roles, and over half said they used research on a daily basis to inform decisions, provide background or balance and learn lessons from other countries. Respondents in this study, led by Caroline Kenny and published by the Parliamentary Office for Science and Technology in 2017, also said that the credibility of research was a key factor they assessed, to ensure they were using what they described as 'authoritative sources'.

More cynically, however, politicians in Kenny's survey also admitted that they used research for political purposes to score points over their opponents. Paul Cairney has written extensively about the politics of evidence use, and there is a legitimate concern that politicians might be using your research to legitimise policy positions or interventions they were already planning to carry out. In most cases, there is nothing wrong with the evidence that is used, but the way in which it is used may leave a lot to be desired, for example, selectively drawing on studies that support a particular position rather than using evidence synthesis or representing contradictory studies where evidence is mixed. In this scenario, the researcher is used as a political pawn. Unless you are convinced that the evidence base for your policy suggestion is sound, there is a danger that your reputation could be called into question when others highlight more robust, contradictory evidence, especially if this later evidence is based on evidence synthesis and your suggestions were based on a single study.

Even when research is used legitimately to support policy, there is often a significant amount of politics involved in the process. If your research happens to align with current political trajectories, then the evidence suggests you are more likely to achieve impact. On the other hand, if you are researching the benefits of immigration in a country that has elected a right-wing government that is 'clamping down' on immigration, you are unlikely to ever get a fair hearing for your research from members of government and the administration serving them (though there may be people opposing the government who may be interested in talking to you). I have worked with colleagues from education around the world who complain that wherever they are based, education policy is rarely informed by research, and whether your research has impact will depend on the whims of ministers and public opinion, no matter how hard you try to communicate your latest findings. Indeed, research published by Katherine Smith and Ellen Stewart in 2016 in the *Journal of Social Policy* showed that in social policy, research that was critical of current policies was only found among the lowest scoring impacts in the UK's 2014 Research Excellence Framework.

Policy impacts happen when research evidence and political will align. This means achieving policy impacts is highly unpredictable and often means playing the long game. The current chief executive, minister or government might not be willing to listen to your evidence, but perhaps their successor will, or perhaps you can identify others who might be able to use your evidence more disruptively to alter the course of policy? I will discuss some of these strategies further in Chapter 4.

Less cynically however, there are a host of other reasons why policy colleagues engage with researchers, which can present significant opportunities for impact. For example, working with researchers can save significant amounts of time, providing rapid access to evidence or evidence-based opinion to help guide decision-making rapidly, when there is insufficient time or resources to review the literature or commission new research. Research is often commissioned to solve a targeted policy problem, identify new policy options or provide evidence for the likely effectiveness of a range of known options under different future scenarios. Research may, for example, focus on the technical feasibility of policy options in policy and practice, given a range of constraints, such as predicted climate change or funding constraints, or it may investigate the social acceptability of policy options to different populations. Different policy colleagues will engage with research for different reasons, depending on their role. For example, ministers may be more motivated to advance the political agenda of their government than backbenchers from their party and opposition parties who may be more interested in using research to scrutinise, improve or oppose policies. Evidence analysts, Chief Scientific Advisors and their teams may be more interested in your methods, data and the technical feasibility of the policy options you have studied, whereas policy officials and strategy teams may be more interested in your results, conclusions and the political feasibility of your ideas. As a researcher, you can provide evidence to support scrutiny and actually get draft legislation changed or dropped altogether.

RESPONSIBLE, STRATEGIC AND PRACTICAL POLICY IMPACT

It has never been more important for researchers to engage with policy, as governments around the world tackle increasingly complex, uncertain and interlinked challenges. However, there are a surprising number of barriers you will have to overcome if you want to use your research to influence policy. According to Vitae's 2021 Culture, Employment and

Development in Academic Research Survey, 61% of researchers in the UK say that they would like to get involved in policy. However, 47% say they do not have time to develop their research skills. Moreover, there is increasing disillusionment among researchers, with a 2020 Wellcome Trust survey reporting that 75% of UK researchers think their creativity is being stifled by the need to generate impact from their research. We need a new approach to engaging with a policy that engages with the values and intrinsic motivations of researchers, whether or not these align with the values and extrinsic incentives of the research systems and governments they work under.

However, existing books on policy engagement for researchers have a number of limitations. Many focus on engaging with the apparatus of government in a single country, which is instantly problematic for researchers whose work is international in scope and significance. Most of the existing literature still presents a simplistic picture of the policy cycle and the role of evidence in policy development and implementation. In these accounts, policy is evidence-based rather than evidence-informed. It is linear and predictable rather than complex and uncertain. And they assume that policy colleagues have decision-making power, when they are actually constrained by many factors, and research is only one of many inputs to the decisions they make.

Most books are targeted at consultants, think tanks, third-sector organisations and industry lobbyists, and so they do not consider the many unique challenges faced by researchers. For example, researchers from different disciplinary traditions can have very different ways of defining knowledge and assessing what counts as evidence, which can significantly influence how they define and practise responsible policy engagement. Most research is inherently complex and often includes many uncertainties, compared to the average consultancy project. This presents unique challenges for researchers around whether or not to attempt to inform policy, and if they do decide to engage, they have to think carefully about how they will communicate complexity and uncertainty.

There are other more practical considerations that researchers have to take into account when working with policy. When policy engagement goes wrong, your mistakes may be very visible publicly, leading to career-threatening impacts on academic reputation and mental health.

Many approaches to policy engagement require a significant ongoing time investment, which may not be compatible with the pressures of an academic post, especially as an early career researcher (ECR). Despite growing pressure to demonstrate policy impact from funders and institutions, there are major challenges in collecting the necessary evidence, given issues attributing policy outcomes to specific research findings, time lags and ideological and other factors that are beyond the control of researchers.

Moreover, there are significant challenges faced by younger, female and ethnic minority researchers in gaining policy influence. Most existing approaches to research-policy engagement do not meaningfully integrate equality, diversity or inclusion. Without tackling these issues, policy engagement handbooks effectively enable academic elites to facilitate political elites to make policy without reference to those who will ultimately be affected by the policies when they are implemented. This has the potential to further marginalise vulnerable groups and generate negative unintended consequences from so-called evidence-based approaches to policy. For these reasons, in Part 1, I will propose a new approach to working with policy in which I will suggest that to generate responsible policy impacts, you need to work with complexity, navigate relationships and manage power and privilege. This is an approach that is rooted in values of curiosity, humility, reflexivity, openness and empathy. I will create a reflective space in which you can interrogate your values and how these influence both your research and your engagement with policy. You will be able to examine your own power and privilege, and how these shape your perception of policy problems and relevant solutions, enabling you to think more critically about how policies are framed, developed and implemented and the roles you can play.

In Part 2, I will encourage you to explore the tensions between different strategic approaches, modes of engagement and the many different roles you can play as a researcher. Are you actually ready to engage with policy yet, or do you need to invest further in strengthening the evidence-base? Are you more comfortable informing policy, or do you want to pursue a more active, influencing strategy? Do you want to take a pragmatic and constructive approach, working closely with policy colleagues, or do you see your role as questioning the assumptions behind how policy problems have been framed and why certain policy options should be either on or off the table? Do you want to rely on your expertise to achieve change, or do you want to use your power and privilege to include those who have no voice in the policy process? If you abandon the simplistic dream of evidence-based policy and embrace the messy reality of complex policy systems, how will you plan for impact and manage the uncertainty?

Once you have done this critical thinking and chosen the approach that fits best with your research, the policies you seek to influence, your career stage and your values, you are ready to start thinking about the practical tools of policy engagement. In Part 3, you will learn how to write a clear and well-targeted policy brief that communicates uncertainty and either proposes actionable policy options or questions existing options to open up new opportunity spaces. I will discuss how you can co-produce and stress-test policy briefs to make your work both relevant and robust and different ways you can use your policy brief to influence policy. You will consider how you might use infographics and visualisations and how you might develop slide decks and use these to present your research to policy audiences with real impact. I will also consider a number of specific mechanisms for informing and influencing policy, for example, testifying to legislative bodies via inquiries and committees, responding to policy consultations, using policy fellowships, shadowing schemes and internships, policy sprints and engaging in commissioned research for policy bodies, as well as more indirect approaches, like using social and mass media. Finally, I will provide you with methods to evaluate and evidence your policy impact. But before we get to any of this, I first need to explain a few core concepts. What actually is policy impact anyway?

Part 1
Responsible policy impact

CHAPTER 2

Policy as research impact

Not all policies are informed by evidence from research, and few can be shown to have arisen primarily from research. To understand how research can influence policy, it is necessary to first ask what we mean by policy? Who are these elusive people called policymakers that everyone talks about? And how can we claim any of what happens as a result of our engagement as impact?

WHAT IS POLICY AND WHO ARE THESE ELUSIVE POLICYMAKERS?

Broadly speaking, a policy is any course of action that is proposed or adopted by an organisation in pursuit of a goal. While 'public policy' usually describes the work of government, it is worth distinguishing between types of action and types of governance. Types of action include making a policy statement, passing legislation or delivering a public service, and types of governance include the various ways policy can be influenced, made and delivered by a large number of governmental and non-governmental organisations. Indeed, half the battle of seeking policy influence is to identify with whom to engage and when. Some research might influence ministerial thinking in central government; other research might engage with local networks of organisations that influence and deliver policy.

In other words, it is always worth considering who the 'policymakers' are. This term is often used loosely to mean anyone from a junior evidence analyst to a government minister, with the implication that these people 'make' policy. In reality, in any democracy the policy-making process is far more complex, involving both politicians and civil servants, as they engage with others who provide policy ideas and evidence.

Similarly, you will often hear people referring to 'the policy community' as though it is a fixed group of people who all know each other and have

DOI: 10.4324/9781003494942-3

the power to make policy. In reality, policy is developed and shaped by diverse and dynamic networks of people, who are often unaware of what people in other policy teams are doing. They sometimes have limited understanding of the issues they are working on and have even more limited control over the policy environment within which they are working. These include members of parliament (in government and opposition), civil servants working in government departments, staff working for government agencies, quasi-governmental organisations and other delivery bodies (such as schools and police forces), charities and other third-sector organisations, think tanks, lobbyists, consultants and academic researchers, to name just a few.

These different people and organisations move in and out of different policy networks as issues come on and off the political agenda and come in and out of public debate. As a result, rather than trying to reach a policy team directly, you may instead work with someone in a government agency or third-sector organisation who already has a strong relationship with the relevant team and is more likely to be able to get the key points from your research across to them in a way that is relevant, efficient and effective (more on this in Chapter 5).

At this point, it is important to allay any fears you may have about the idea of 'influencing' policy as manipulating or lobbying. As a researcher, it is essential that the research you hope might contribute towards policy meets the standards of rigour in your discipline, typically including peer-review, and where possible including evidence synthesis beyond the findings of your current project. When I refer to 'influencing' policy, I am referring to proactive knowledge exchange with relevant people, who may (or may not) go on to develop policy based on your research. This contrasts with 'informing' policy, where I am referring to a more reactive process of transferring knowledge and making evidence available when requested. Clearly, there is room for both informing and influencing policy, and the latter often follows from the former.

There are, however, political actors who may be seeking to manipulate policy to benefit one group over another. And there are many ways in which members of policy networks may themselves be manipulated. But rather than learning these 'dark arts', I suggest instead that you are aware of some of the more common traps that researchers can fall into, leading them to behave in ways that are inadvertently manipulative. For example:

- You should avoid focusing narrowly on your own research at the expense of the wider evidence base (especially when there is conflicting evidence and even if your funder has asked you to only focus on the work they funded);
- Metaphors and analogies can be useful to help explain complex concepts to non-specialists, but be careful that you are not inadvertently oversimplifying or misleading people;
- Beware that numbers, graphs and maps can imply that evidence is precise, accurate and certain; when in reality it may be none of these things, and your attempts to explain the uncertainty may be lost as your statistic is quoted and requoted by others (I will discuss some of the traps you can fall into when using infographics and visualisations in Chapter 11); and
- Attempt to see the issues you are researching and the policy options you are developing through the eyes of multiple groups within society so that you don't inadvertently accept a dominant framing of an issue that plays into the interests of powerful groups, while marginalising others.

As Paul Cairney wrote in his book, *The Politics of Policy Analysis* (2021, p. 77), 'evidence does not speak for itself. Instead, people engage in effective communication and persuasion to assign meaning to the evidence.'

WHEN IS POLICY A RESEARCH IMPACT?

I have defined research impact as 'demonstrable and/or perceptible benefits to individuals, groups, organisations and society (including human and non-human entities in the present and future) that are causally linked (necessarily or sufficiently) to research' (in my 2021 article in *Research Policy* – see Further reading).

However, policy impacts are unusual. Public policy distributes unequal benefits and burdens across populations, sometimes by design and sometimes as an unintended consequence. As such, while it is useful to pursue a normative definition of *impact on policy* as seeking to help deliver public benefits, you should keep a critical eye on who actually benefits versus who ends up being disadvantaged in some way when a policy is implemented.

Therefore, when considering whether a policy change represents a *research* impact, we need to consider three things:

- The significance of the policy and its outcomes in terms of the degree to which the policy is beneficial, and for whom;
- Its reach, both geographically and in terms of the diversity or importance of the groups it benefits; and
- The extent to which the policy can be attributed to research.

While most impact typologies consider research-informed policy to be a research impact in and of itself, the significance of this impact will depend on whether the policy is actually implemented, resourced and enforced and leads to anticipated public benefits. This is not straightforward to determine, as we will discuss in Chapter 5, as a benefit for one group within society may compromise the interests of other, opposing groups. Not only may there be winners and losers, but in her 2012 article in *Policy Studies*, Diane Stone showed that the same population can report contradictory perceptions of the desirability of policies, supporting one policy and its complete opposite in answer to different questions in the same poll.

Ultimately, to claim a significant policy impact, you will want evidence of the benefits arising from the application of that policy. In most cases, it is sufficient to claim that you helped shape a policy, if you are able to justify why, on the basis of your research, this should deliver public benefits. The significance of the impact will then depend on the nature of the policy change, for example whether you influenced a non-binding strategy or a piece of enforceable legislation, and the significance of that strategy, law or other policy in terms of what it sets out to achieve. For example, adding a new monitoring indicator to a piece of existing water quality regulation that marginally increases its effectiveness is in a different ballpark to introducing a new law that bans the use of a polluting substance all together.

The reach of most policy impacts is jurisdictional, based on the operational limits of the organisation or the national boundaries of the government creating the policy. However, within these geographical boundaries, there is often a more interesting and important story to tell about the diversity of beneficiaries or the way in which a marginalised or vulnerable group is likely to benefit as a result of the new policy.

Attributing any kind of policy change to your own research is a major challenge, and I will tackle this properly in Chapter 13. At this point, it is important to appreciate that the extent to which you can claim significant and far-reaching policy impact with your research will depend on the extent to which you can claim your research actually informed important parts of the policy (even if other researchers and factors not related to research also informed the change). Ultimately, whether your research achieves policy impact is highly unpredictable, and despite your best efforts, a change of government or the ideology of a new minister may mean your evidence never gets used. However, as I will discuss in Chapter 4, there are many different routes you can pursue to reduce this risk. For example, you might switch your attention to a different country, you could work to shape the manifesto of an opposition party or you could start working with a third-sector organisation opposing the current policy, who might be empowered by your evidence and able to affect change, for example through a public campaign.

Context may also affect how the significance and reach of your impact is viewed. If you are working with a government that has a strong reputation for effectively implementing policy, then helping to shape an important new national policy will typically be deemed a significant and far-reaching impact by other researchers. However, if you achieve a similar impact in a state that has limited resources to implement the policy and a history of failed policies in the area you're working in, then claiming that your research shaped a policy might be taken less seriously (and it will be more important to provide evidence of actual change resulting from the policy). Similarly, influencing medical guidelines in countries with well-developed healthcare systems is highly regarded as a policy impact because of the history of these guidelines being applied in clinical practice and delivering benefits to patients. However, people might be less impressed if you influenced a national guideline that involves a medical technology the country can't afford to roll out across its health service.

LOOK FOR IMPACTS ON YOUR PATHWAY TO POLICY OUTCOMES

In addition to considering impacts arising as a result of a new policy, you may also want to consider impacts that occur prior to any policy change. This is important because the policy process often takes much longer than you expect, and having tangible benefits for the people who are hoping for change in the meantime can be important in keeping them engaged and motivated to continue working with you. There are two key types of impact you can look for.

First, you might build understanding or awareness among policy networks or the wider public based on your research. The significance of this will depend on the extent to which a lack of understanding or misconception is problematic and needs to be addressed. Building a research-informed problem statement will enable you to identify the key pieces of information and knowledge you need to target and increase the likelihood that you achieve a meaningful change in understanding or awareness that addresses the need you have identified. In many cases, this will be identified for you via a consultation or call for evidence in which civil servants identify key knowledge gaps and evidence needs that they would like to learn more about. In other cases, you might identify a knowledge gap that nobody is aware of, for example a negative unintended consequence of a proposed policy. In this case, you will need to reach out in a very targeted way to ensure that the relevant policy team are aware of your research and its implications so that they can resolve the issue you have identified. At this stage, all they may be able to do is to put the policy on hold until they can commission research to resolve the issue you have identified. But whether or not it has yet been resolved, the fact that you brought this to their attention is clearly beneficial, and so this can be viewed an impact because you have helped avoid negative impacts.

In other cases, your goal may be to influence public debate and raise awareness about an issue broadly so that in time this will influence policy debate as politicians respond to the resulting rise in public attention. The significance of this impact will depend on the significance of the change in understanding and awareness, both in terms of the extent to which information has been learned and retained as knowledge and the extent to which this changes how they think, potentially influencing attitudes or more deeply held values and beliefs. For example, you may be able to tackle biases and assumptions, leading to a more favourable attitude towards a technology or policy option among policy teams or politicians or among members of the public. Or you may be able to spot opportunities to transform beliefs into action, getting people to act on their existing beliefs rather than attempting to change their beliefs entirely.

Second, you may build capacity within policy networks or publics. Broadly speaking, there are two types of capacity building you might achieve. On the one hand, your research might connect people to each other who previously did not know or interact with each other or who did not trust each other. These may be individuals within policy networks or organisations and groups. As a result of your research, there is now enduring connectivity, which can enable these groups to access information and resources that were previously unavailable to them. Now when a problem arises, they know exactly who to contact who might be able to help, and as a result, they may adapt or respond more rapidly and effectively to that problem. However, before there is any evidence of improved cooperation, it is beneficial and hence impactful that these people are connected to each other because they have the capacity through these new networks to respond more effectively to change or exploit opportunities that would otherwise have been unavailable. In policy networks, this can provide civil servants with access to data or expertise that was otherwise not available to them, enabling them to achieve new policy goals or respond more effectively in a policy crisis, in collaboration with those in their new networks. Such networks might enable small organisations or disempowered groups to connect with each other, mobilise other networks, share resources and expertise and effect changes that would otherwise not be possible.

The other way you can build capacity on your pathway to policy impacts is to enable those you are working with to gain new skills or capabilities, for example by making your data available via a user-friendly database or creating a user interface for your computer model that can enable non-experts to interrogate your data or model for themselves. Alternatively, you may provide training, equipping your policy colleagues or members of organisations working with important publics to do things they couldn't do before.

You will notice that each of these early impacts is not just engagement processes; they meet my definition of impact as a benefit. It is therefore crucial to be clear on the difference between impact and engagement, to ensure the time you spend engaging with policy networks actually drives benefits and avoids wasting your time and the time of your policy colleagues. Writing a consultation response or policy brief is not - in itself - a policy impact – neither is leading a high-level policy seminar or giving evidence to a committee or inquiry. Each of these activities is an important way of engaging with policy, as we will explore further in Part 3. However, in and of themselves, they do not benefit anyone - yet. In the worst-case scenario, your policy brief might not be read by anyone, your consultation response might be completely misunderstood and the oral evidence you delivered might be ignored. In these cases, there is no change, or there could be a negative unintended consequence (in the case of being misunderstood), so you cannot claim any of this activity as impact.

This is not to denigrate the importance of these activities; without good engagement, you will never stand a chance of achieving any policy impact. But it is the first step, and you will need to keep pursuing your objective of delivering tangible benefits long after your first engagement. You will need to monitor your success as you go and change tack when it looks like your approach isn't working. Successful policy engagement takes time and perseverance.

CHAPTER **3**

A new approach to working with policy

Traditional approaches to policy impact run into problems when we take a simplistic or overly instrumental approach to either policy or impact. In spite of the best intentions and hardest work, many attempts to use research in policy settings have limited success. For example, the research that underpinned 'green revolution' policies to mechanise and industrialise agriculture to provide food security across Africa in the 1970s were based on sound research that had previously only been applied in the Global North. More recent approaches to tackle food insecurity via genetically modified (GM) crops have run into similar problems despite the fact that they were based on rigorous research. In their new setting, tractors broke down and parts were not available to fix them. GM crops were more productive but had to be used with specific (and expensive) herbicides and pesticides, and harvested seeds were not fertile, so farmers couldn't collect seeds for next year's crop, having to buy new seed each year.

There can be significant time lags between research funding applications to the publication of findings (typically three to five years). Given that few current governments will still be in place five years from now, this is a problem. Most policy colleagues are looking for answers to questions within hours or days (it is rare that they can wait weeks). Even one year is too long for most policy teams to wait for an answer. This means that to help policy colleagues, most of us will need to rely on existing literature and expertise to meet current needs. While we are doing this, we have opportunities to building trusting relationships with individual policy colleagues and our reputation with wider policy teams (given that most individuals will move to new positions over the course of a

DOI: 10.4324/9781003494942-4

research project). This will then position us to identify relevant windows of opportunity when our research is eventually ready.

However, we may have to wait many years for these windows of opportunity to open, and as time progresses, we may have to do further research to adapt our work to changing policy contexts. As a result, studies of the most impactful case studies submitted to the UK's Research Excellence Framework and Hong Kong's Research Assessment Exercise suggest a further time lag between publication and actual impact of at least another decade. In some cases, researchers may still be waiting long after that for a hoped-for change in government or ideology that might align with their research. For example, as English immigration policy has tightened over successive decades, I have watched colleagues with evidence of the benefits of immigration make their own journeys to more welcoming countries like Scotland, which wants to increase immigration rates. Finally, when you do eventually achieve some level of policy change, there will be so many contributing factors that it may be impossible to prove that you played a role.

THERE IS NO SUCH THING AS EVIDENCE-BASED POLICY

As if it weren't already hard enough to achieve policy impacts, many researchers fall into traps that are known to hinder the use of their work in policy. Perhaps the most insidious of these traps is a belief in evidence-based policy. There is no such thing as 'evidence-based policy' – only 'evidence-informed policy' – since policy is, and should be, driven by other factors, such as the professional experience and judgement of civil servants and the values of their elected political masters. If researchers were in charge of countries then, we might do evidence-based policy, but this would no longer be democracy, and evidence from any research conference suggests to me that we'd be no better at agreeing with each other than our politicians. Your task as a researcher is to make your evidence available to the right people at the right time, to help inform their decision-making, and not to actually make the decisions. Decision-making is the role of elected politicians, or for the smaller decisions, civil servants.

You or I might presume that academic research is an infinitely preferable input to policy decisions than lobbying from corporations, but inputs from business (indeed from any group in society) are not only just as valid but also they are often just as persuasive, if not more so. Chris Cook, a Deputy Director in the UK's Government Office for Science, was quoted by Tim Vorley and colleagues in their 2022 book *How to Engage Policymakers with Your Research*: The Art of Informing and Impacting Policy, saying, 'Academic research is one of several sources of advice to Government. Input from academics can feel quite unstructured compared to input from business, where there are often dedicated representative bodies for specific sectors'.

If our task is to get our research to the people who can make decisions, then simply publishing your research open access is not enough. There is a difference between your research being available in this way and it actually reaching those who could most benefit from engaging with it. There is also a difference between your research being available and understandable; the majority of open-access papers are unintelligible to anyone outside the discipline in which they were published. I will consider a range of ways you might make your research more understandable to different policy audiences later in the book.

Once your evidence has reached someone who might be able to use it, and they have understood your findings, it will be just one of many inputs to any policy decision. Not all research is useful as evidence, and not all evidence is research-based. In addition to other researchers and findings, there will be other arguments vying for the attention of the policy colleagues who are interrogating your research. These may include moral and ideological arguments that in the view of the policymaker may demand a course of action that directly contradicts your evidence. Unconventional though this may sound, there is an argument that I will unpack later in this chapter, for identifying and representing these perspectives yourself and presenting them alongside your research evidence. These concerns may arise from the very people you hope that the policy will benefit, and so it is possible to argue that by representing these voices, we have the potential to democratise policy-making. For example, Box 3.1 describes how researchers from the University of Leeds used social science to give voice to marginalised children, enabling their perspectives to be heard and help shape policy.

Finally, in addition to inputs from research, others with a legitimate claim to comment on the policy and their own professional judgement, your policy colleagues will be constrained by the environment in which they are working. For example, there may be both opportunities and

Box 3.1 Amplifying the voices of children in poverty.

Dr Gill Main's research aimed to put the experiences of children and families living in poverty at the heart of the UK poverty debate and help reach the ultimate goal of ending poverty for all.

Dr Main surveyed families and partnered with schools, a local authority and charities to bridge the gap between academic research and society. This research collated and amplified the knowledge of families with first-hand experience of living in poverty, reducing feelings of stigma or shame associated with their experiences. Main has changed the policy rhetoric to better represent the real-world experiences of those living in poverty.

Families with first-hand experience of living in poverty felt heard and gained confidence and self-esteem; many found a new way of understanding poverty as a social injustice and not as their personal failing. Main's research also changed how policies are designed in the city of Leeds to address poverty, ensuring the voices of children and families living in poverty are listened to. This research has helped local authorities, charities and advocates to develop a better understanding of poverty issues and to design interventions to help work towards a fairer society for everyone.

constraints arising from the political and institutional context in which they find themselves. Ideologies, norms or previous policies may influence how a problem is perceived and framed and constrain the range of options deemed politically feasible. Equally, the political context may present windows of opportunity as a result of elections or the political imperative to respond to a crisis or some other focusing event. I will discuss some of these complexities further in Chapter 4 and have summarised the factors influencing policy decisions in Figure 3.1.

Figure 3.1 Factors influencing policy decisions, showing how research is one of a number of factors playing into most decisions.

WE NEED A NEW APPROACH TO IMPACT

Despite these challenges, governments and funders around the world are increasingly incentivising researchers to generate impact from their work. Although this has led to investment in staff, infrastructure and training for impact, it has also added significant pressure to academics who were already struggling to research and teaching expectations. This pressure has resulted in negative unintended consequences; in the UK, a civil servant once told me they were fed up of researchers phoning them up to 'have an impact on me, when I've got a job to do' and where Richard Watermeyer has reported a policy colleague saying, 'I think there's a lot of folks here from both government and parliament who are just getting a bit exhausted, explaining that the role of government is not to add some impact to your study'.

It is not just the system that is broken; it is clear to me that we need a whole new way of doing impact, which focuses more on what I've called 'impact culture', if we want to draw researchers to impact on their terms, motivating them to work with policy because they actually want to. No amount of new incentives will achieve the attitudinal change necessary to make our interactions with policy colleagues more respectful. But I want to suggest that we can go further than simply becoming more respectful, to more deeply understanding the people we work with, their institutions and the system they work in. In so doing, I want to enable you to manage the power and politics that are hidden but inherent in any attempt to advise policy and build trusting relationships that will outlast their current post and your current research project.

YOUR TASK IS TO MANAGE COMPLEXITY, RELATIONSHIPS AND POWER

Most policy impact guides and toolkits present an attractively simple, but I will argue simplistic, model of how to influence policy:

1. Work with policy colleagues to clearly identify a policy problem you can help with;
2. Conduct research or draw on existing work to identify technically and politically feasible solutions to the problem;
3. Use objective criteria and political goals to compare and rank solutions;

4. Conduct research or draw on existing work to predict the likely out-comes of the top-ranked solutions; and
5. Make concise evidence-based recommendations to solve the problem, sharing the pros and cons of each solution and using visual aids to communicate clearly and make the problem seem solvable.

What could possibly be wrong with such a tried-and-tested approach to working with policy? If politics were simple, then such a simple approach might work, but the problem is that reality is a lot more complex:

- What if policy colleagues in different departments (or even in different teams within the same department) see the problem in very different ways?
- What if each of those ways of seeing the problem is a result of assumptions based on previous policies (e.g. posit economic growth as an imperative) and fail to see the problem from the perspective of those who are being negatively impacted by current policies?
- How is the definition of what's politically feasible shaped by the way a government has consistently stereotyped and overlooked the needs of certain populations?
- What if, by only considering options that are politically feasible for the current administration, you might further marginalise the most needy in society?
- Who represents their interests, and do we have a responsibility to share our power as researchers to give voice to those who are rarely heard in the corridors of power?
- Who chooses the supposedly objective criteria for evaluating policy options, and how do these criteria reflect their values and assumptions, leading to biases in decision-making that protect the interests of others with similar values and assumptions?
- Can we ever predict with any accuracy how a policy might play out in a complex system that we do not fully understand?
- What if our policy colleagues don't actually have the power we think they do to either develop or implement policy?
- What if power is decentralised to regional governments and delivery agencies who we aren't talking to, and implementation depends on the unpredictable decisions of countless people as they interact with unknown future events and other drivers of change?

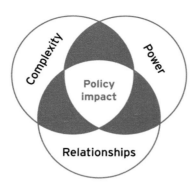

Figure 3.2 Conceptual framework for responsible policy impact.

To suggest that it is as simple as those well-trodden five steps is either hubris or wilful negligence, given the power we have to challenge assumptions and stay involved in the messiness of policy implementation until we actually see the outcomes we seek. Instead, if we want to generate policy impacts responsibly, our task is to manage complexity, relationships and power, as I will explain in the following chapters (Figure 3.2).

By doing this, we are uniquely positioned as researchers, not only to influence policy but also to question assumptions about how policy should be made. Instead of relying on experts like us, we can become experts in connecting our policy colleagues to those who are typically excluded from policy development, giving voice to the marginalised and broadening the democratic as well as the evidential basis of policy. Policy colleagues are trying to balance the need for both evidence and inclusivity in policy-making but do not always have time to review all the most relevant evidence or engage with all the most relevant perspectives from those who might be affected by the policy. By combining the top-down, traditional role of researchers as experts with more bottom-up engagement with affected populations and external organisations pushing for change, researchers have the potential to achieve more responsible impacts. By engaging across policy networks, it becomes possible to join or form alliances with others, spreading the work of achieving policy change and helping researchers formulate more politically feasible proposals that are more likely to work in practice. Given the limited time and resources of many civil service teams and their generalist expertise, we can provide valuable advice outside formal mechanisms like consultations and expert advisory groups and play an important role as part of a wider network of expertise that policy colleagues can call upon. This is particularly important in post-colonial settings, where researchers from former colonial powers often still engage in extractive research practices that deliver research outputs for funders in research-intensive countries that cut out researchers and patronise policy teams in the country that hosted them. I will discuss how we can decolonise 'helicopter' research practices like this in Chapter 6, but the issue goes much deeper than the geopolitics of colonialism, to a superior, entitled mindset that many researchers have when interacting with policy teams in their own countries.

Many of us are unaware of these attitudes and beliefs until challenged. But rather than confront you or guilt you into examining yourself, I want you to dig deep, into five values-based principles that will enable you to start instinctively managing complexity, power and relationships in new ways:

- Curiosity;
- Humility;
- Reflexivity;
- Openness; and
- Empathy.

We need to be as curious about the policy system and its people, institutions and history as we are about our research. We should be humble enough to admit the limits of our own expertise so we can learn from others, embracing uncertainty and helping our policy colleagues adapt as policy experiments unfold in the real world. We should reflect on our own position in the policy system, including the different roles we can play, and our own prejudices and power. We need to be open to multiple perspectives and ways of seeing the world, if we are to keep learning, make our evidence useful and inclusive and democratise decision-making. Finally, we need to build trusting, long-term relationships with policy colleagues and others in our wider policy networks, including those with very different values and goals to us, so we critically debate ideas and facilitate cooperation across and beyond government, spreading the workload and staying with our ideas from policy development through to implementation.

TAKE YOUR COURAGE IN YOUR HANDS

But will these policy colleagues reach out to *you*? As Richard Watermeyer suggested in his book *Competitive accountability in academic life*, in the UK at least, many of the academics advising Government are older, white men, often with the title of Professor. However, if you do not fit this stereotype, the good news is that policy colleagues are just looking for someone credible who can give them quick and easy access to robust evidence, and that could be you, even if you are an early career researcher (ECR).

If you are questioning this, then you are not alone. One of the most common reasons that the early career colleagues I train are not engaging with policy is that they are worried they do not have enough knowledge or expertise. As soon as they start engaging with policy colleagues, they begin to feel like they shouldn't be there, and the longer they engage, the more likely they are to be 'found out' as a fraud. Often described as 'imposter syndrome', this feeling is also common among more senior colleagues because the more you know, the more you appreciate how much you don't know.

My first experience of policy-induced imposter syndrome occurred during a phone call with a government economist when I myself was an ECR. The economist, Helen Dunn, told me I was their 'go to' person on payments for ecosystem services. I instantly had an attack of imposter syndrome and instinctively wanted to tell them how worried they should be that I was the best person they had found, when there were so many others with so much more expertise than me. Although I was working on the topic at the time, I hadn't published anything relevant at that point, and I was very far from being an economist (I can't even do maths). But I stopped myself from voicing these doubts, when I realised that most of my more senior colleagues didn't see this as important work and wouldn't make time for Helen. However, I had been able to get their help to answer Helen's questions and had conveyed what I had learned in good time to Helen in a format that she could use. When I didn't know anyone who could help answer Helen's questions, I would go to the literature and summarise key points, or I would tell her I couldn't help. I was accessible and helpful, and I was credible enough. Those are all the qualifications you need to advise someone like Helen. While Helen was a lowly evidence analyst at the time, she was often briefing ministers or writing new policy, giving me opportunities for impact that are rare for an ECR.

A lack of academic expertise and confidence are two of the most common concerns I hear from ECRs who come to my influencing policy training course at Fast Track Impact. These are valid concerns, especially if you are planning to engage in higher risk, influencing strategies, like media interviews, webinars or seminars, where you might be expected to have answers to questions beyond your immediate, typically narrow expertise. It takes courage in these settings to admit that you don't know the answer to a seemingly simple question, but it is essential that you do because even hazarding an educated guess could have terrible consequences if you are wrong. In most other settings however, it is easy enough to tell someone you'll get back to them with some answers later (remember to find out how much later is too late for their purposes though). Confidence comes with experience, and it is better that you stay in your comfort zone, if that protects your reputation and mental health, until you feel ready. As a more experienced academic, I find it easier to navigate questions in webinars and seminars than I used to, but I still refuse live media interviews (on the rare occasion I'm asked) because they terrify me.

If terror is the emotion that comes to mind as you think about engaging with policy, then you are not alone. Many of the people I train find it nerve-wracking enough presenting their research to peers at conferences, let alone to people who might ask trick questions to score political points. Personally, I have suffered from anxiety for many years, and one of the places I'm most likely to panic is on stage. I've learned strategies that work most of the time for in-person and online events, but I'm not going to chance it with a live media interview. I don't need that kind of stress in my life. I say this not to elicit pity but to legitimise 'no' as a valid answer to an opportunity to make a difference. Nobody else knows your context, and they don't have to know your reasons why. So, don't let anyone pressure you into engaging in ways that make you feel uncomfortable. There are many effective ways you can engage that do not require public speaking; in fact, most of the policy impacts I've been involved with have been based on informal, one-to-one conversations.

I also want to demonstrate that it is possible to do policy work, even if you are an introvert or suffer from anxiety; it might just cost you more than it would an extrovert. To make this possible, I have had to work on my imposter syndrome, which can be particularly acute in policy settings, given my potential for both great good and devastating harm, depending on how I use the opportunity. Like me, you might be asking yourself, 'who am I to be advising national policy?' And if by this, you mean to say that you're not the world expert, then of course, you're right. But you are you, with all the credibility that comes from being a researcher from your institution, and as Helen showed me, the only other things you need are to be accessible and helpful. As I explained in greater depth in my last book, *Impact Culture*, people experience imposter syndrome in direct proportion to the gap between their perception of their own expertise and the world's perception of them. That's one of the reasons why working with policy provokes feelings of fear in so many researchers; being billed as the 'expert', or in Helen's case as her 'go to person', makes you aware of everything that you are not. I wasn't an economist, and I hadn't published anything yet. You know all the gaps in your knowledge and the limits to your expertise, and yet people come to you, redolent with hope, expecting you to have answers.

Of course, if imposter syndrome is driven by the gap between your perception of yourself and how the world sees you, then the treatment is obvious. First, you need to manage people's expectations, explaining the limits of your knowledge, your lack of experience or the other constraints that will make it difficult to stray far beyond your current, narrow expertise. That's the easy bit. The more challenging task is to work on your own perception of your value and worth as a researcher. It may help to get new skills and find low-risk settings in which you can practise things like public speaking. One of the most valuable training sessions I attended was with a voice coach who specialised in public speaking, which I then practised in lectures and conference talks before applying them to higher risk, policy talks. As an ECR at the time, part of my strategy was to recognise the value my colleagues could bring to the table, which I had access to, and my ability to use academic search engines. I didn't need to claim that I was anything I was not.

This is why I tell my PhD students that they too can start engaging with policy colleagues, as long as they have completed your literature review and understand what they have written. Even now, having published over 200 articles, I am rarely able to provide policy advice based on my own research alone. Like you, I rely on evidence from the literature to supplement my own knowledge. As long as you trust your sources, you can provide policy advice based on existing evidence, without ever having published anything of your own on the subject. In fact, the first ever policy advice I was asked to provide came as a PhD student in Botswana. I was working alongside a United Nations (UN) programme and had noticed that their staff were breaking all the rules of how to conduct good interviews and focus groups. I could see their mistakes because I'd been given training in social science methods at the University of Leeds, where I was studying. So, I shared a copy of the University's training slides with the programme director. He was instantly enthusiastic. 'We've never had any training in this', he told me. 'None of us have a clue what we're doing, but its clear that you know more than us. Can you deliver this training to the team?' I instantly apologised and explained that I was just a PhD student and had only just learned this stuff myself. But he persisted. Clearly, I knew more than they did. I trusted my sources, in this case, my colleagues in Leeds rather than the literature, and so I took my courage in my hands and agreed to train them. I had started my journey into working with policy.

This journey from terror to growing confidence, in which under-achievers over-estimate their competence and high-achievers underestimate their expertise, has been described as the 'Dunning-Kruger effect', after a study published by David Dunning and Justin Kruger in 1999 in the *Journal of Personality and Social Psychology* (Figure 3.3). I regularly meet lobbyists who have remained for much of their career on the peak of 'Mount Stupid', driven primarily by their values or paymasters. Blind to their own ignorance, they push policy proposals that could have disastrous consequences, if adopted. Most researchers know significantly more than these lobbyists, and if they were engaging in the conversation, they could quickly point out the obvious flaws and inaccuracies to their policy colleagues. The irony, however, is that most researchers give 'Mount Stupid' a wide berth and, instead, head straight to the 'Valley of Despair'. They know that they are not the 'Guru' in their field yet, but they know more than the policy colleagues who are looking for answers and more than the lobbyists who pretend to have answers. Although I have gained in confidence as I have learned more, it has been my experience working with policy more than my expertise that has emboldened me to

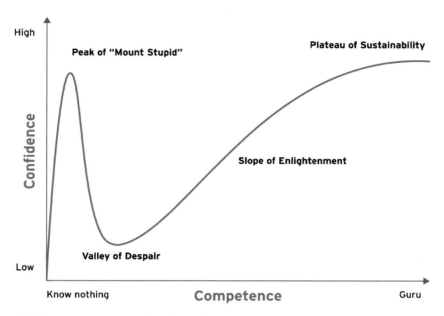

Figure 3.3 The Dunning-Kruger effect (licensed under a Creative Commons CC0 1.0 Universal Public Domain Dedication).

engage more. Personally, I don't know who the supposed 'gurus' are in my field, and I would question the wisdom of giving anyone that label, if it means people unquestioning accept their advice. Indeed, Justine Lacey and colleagues, writing in *Nature Climate Change* in 2018 argued that placing too much trust in researchers can be detrimental to good policy-making when 'blind faith' leads to complacency, favouritism or a lack of objectivism or prevents people pursuing more innovative ideas. I feel deeply uncomfortable when I am introduced to audiences as the 'impact guru' because that's not how I see myself, knowing everything that I do not know about impact. We are all on the 'slope of enlightenment', and I hope that my curiosity will mean that I never plateaux, comfortable in my guru status. If you are waiting until you reach guru status before engaging with policy, you might never start, and you might deny the world the many insights you already have.

Overall, of course, it is legitimate and understandable to experience fear or reluctance to engage with policy networks, particularly when the outcomes are so unpredictable. What if you get asked a question you can't answer? What if your research is cherry-picked, distorted and used to justify repressive policies in your name? Many such scenarios may be running through your mind at this point. I cannot entirely de-risk the process of engaging with policy, but I can recommend skills that can help (see Chapter 8 for ways to reduce the risks of policy engagement).

Finally, it is important to note that even if you can overcome imposter syndrome, there may be a number of other life circumstances that may constrain your capacity to engage with policy. For example, those with caring responsibilities may not be able to travel to engage with policy colleagues in person at meetings or events or to provide oral evidence in committees and hearings. In most cases, there is an option to join electronically, but building empathic connection with people you have never met in person is much harder than meeting them face-to-face. All researchers considering policy engagement have to also consider the demands on their time, but if you work part-time, this may be particularly challenging. Although there are now a range of incentives and institutional support for researchers who want to engage with policy, career progression for ECRs is still predicated primarily on publications and research funding rather than evidence of impact. This may make it harder for ECRs to justify spending significant amounts of time in policy engagement.

Ultimately, however, finding time for any task as a researcher is about priorities, so the final question in this module is to ask yourself why you are doing this course, and why engaging with policy is important to you? What parts of your identity and which values are you able to express by engaging in policy work? What is the sense of purpose and meaning you derive from this sort of work? Goal hierarchy theory suggests that once you are clear on the values and identities you are expressing by engaging with policy, you will instinctively prioritise policy tasks with whatever time you have available, deprioritising, delegating or truncating other tasks that are less well aligned with your identity and values (see Kerrie Unsworth's accessible review of this theory in her co-authored 2015 article in *Journal of Organisational Behaviour*). Before you move to Chapter 4, I encourage you to reflect on your reasons for wanting to engage with policy and why this is important to you. Reflect on how this sort of work might enable you to express identities and values and provide you with a sense of meaning or purpose.

CHAPTER **4**

Working with complexity

The complexity of most real-world policy environments means that those who are supposedly making policy often have limited control over the decisions that are ultimately made. These may be as much about the political system, previous policies, current ideologies, the formal and informal rules and norms of their institution, events of the day and the knowledge, experience and biases of the individual decision-maker as they are about the actual policy options on the table. What gets policy attention may be as much to do with what is in the news (which may of course be manipulated by those seeking to push issues up the policy agenda). As a result, important issues may be crowded out by other more urgent and politically salient issues (or be minimised as unimportant those who seek to maintain the status quo).

This complexity presents a real challenge to researchers who want to engage with policy. How can you plan for impact when you have no idea who might have decision-making power at any given point in time, what the policy problem is and what factors might alter the nature or framing of the problem, or the relevance and viability of the solutions you have in mind?

MANAGING COMPLEXITY: THE OBJECTIVIST APPROACH

Objectivist approaches to policy-making would suggest that we need to understand and adapt to each of the many factors that make policy systems so complex and unpredictable, if we want to influence decision-makers. Proponents of this approach suggest that in doing so, it is possible to develop an influencing strategy in which we can influence multiple individual rational choices, which will ultimately aggregate to deliver the policy change we want to see.

DOI: 10.4324/9781003494942-5

I used to subscribe to this model, working with teams of researchers to develop complex models that attempted to capture as much of this complexity as possible, to identify specific places in the system where policy change could deliver better outcomes. Based on Donella Meadows's (1999) concept of 'leverage points', a small change in the right part of a complex system can have a cascade effect on the rest of the system, leading to significant shifts in outcomes. The concept is innately attractive, given the potential for one small policy change to act as a miracle cure across a complex system. But given the complexity of these systems, it is very easy to propose simple changes that can go badly wrong. After publishing his 1971 book, *World Dynamics*, Jay Forrester was invited by the Club of Rome to investigate how major global problems like poverty, environmental destruction, urban deterioration and unemployment were related and how they might be solved. He created a system dynamics model that identified a clear leverage point: economic growth. However, as we have subsequently seen, the economic benefits of growth are easier to measure than the costs, which ultimately fuel environmental destruction, poverty and many of the other problems that growth seeks to solve. As a result, Donella Meadows suggests that if we're looking for leverage points, the sorts of things we need to target first are the mindsets and paradigms out of which the system arises. If we can transcend these paradigms, we can question the goals that the system seeks to achieve and how it is organised to achieve those goals. As a result, many analysts now suggest that what is needed is much slower growth, different kinds of growth and perhaps no growth or degrowth, to refocus our economies on delivering wellbeing within environmental limits.

Nevertheless, the lure of 'a model everything' remains strong to this day. After all, who wouldn't want a tool that can identify simple changes in policy that can change everything and predict exactly how your new policy will change the world? Drawn inexorably to this promise, I have worked with modellers from across the social and natural sciences to build various kinds of systems models. Some were expert based, drawing on conversations with experts to create causal loop diagrams. Others were driven by relationships between variables that we found in the literature, including the integration of process-based models of different sub-systems using Bayesian mathematics. Some were driven by empirical data, based on interviews with farmers who became 'agents' in our agent-based models of human behaviour, responding to new policies in different ways depending on their age, educational status, farm type, and what their neighbours were doing. In a number of projects, we then linked these models of human behaviour to models that showed how the decisions farmers made in response to a policy would play out in terms of the ecology, water and carbon across landscapes, integrating insights from process-based models of the natural environment. Ultimately, the idea is that by understanding as much as possible about how a problem or policy might play out in the real world, it is possible to design policies that are adapted to real-world settings. Of course, the problem is that the real world is highly unpredictable.

Our saving grace was the fact that most of our models didn't actually work that well, so we were too nervous to actually make concrete policy recommendations, in case we were wrong. Models are only ever as good as the data you feed them with or, in the absence of data, the evidence underpinning the assumptions you use to structure your model. In one case, I realised our attempt to model an upland system with any accuracy was doomed during a team meeting about six months into the project. Many uplands in the UK are dominated by a dwarf shrub called heather, and Heather is also a popular girls name in the country. We had hired a Post-Doctoral Research Assistant from a very different part of the world who had never been to the UK before starting the job with us. She had been developing a framework to link our agent-based model to a model of ecological dynamics and was not making much progress. During this meeting, she has a sudden moment of insight. Her eyes lit up as she told everyone, 'I've just realised something'. Everyone looked at her as she revealed to us that she had been wondering since the start of the project which member of the team was called Heather, but she had just realised that heather was a plant. At that point, I realised that we were never going to be able to model this system. We needed a new plan. Instead of trying to predict how the system would respond to changes in agricultural policy, we would use our models alongside existing literature and the voices of the farmers we had interviewed to develop plausible scenarios of how the system *might* change. We would explain that all of these might be completely wrong, but we hoped that our scenarios would stimulate discussion, to help our policy colleagues think more deeply about the instruments they were developing.

Ultimately, the idea behind the objectivist approach and projects like this is that by understanding as much as possible about how a problem or policy might play out in the real world, it is possible to design policies that are adapted to real-world settings. Of course, the problem is that the real world is highly unpredictable, which leads me to the systems approach.

POLICY WINDOWS AND THIRD-ORDER SYSTEM CHANGE: THE SYSTEMS APPROACH

In contrast to the objectivist approach, an alternative approach is to view policy as a system that has unpredictable emergent properties. The complexity of the system makes it impossible to objectively predict how any policy might ultimately work out. Therefore, rather than trying to understand everything in sufficient detail to be able to make a grand policy plan, smaller, more incremental changes are sought, until a major shock in the policy system (e.g. a disaster or an election) makes opens windows of opportunity for bigger changes.

A decade after our failed 'Heather model', I came back with systems evaluation expert Pete Barbrook-Johnson to see what had actually happened and how the instrument we helped our policy colleagues design had actually worked in reality. The systems diagram we created is too complex to reproduce here in any detail, but you can see it in the paper, which I've included in Further Reading. It took ten years from the end of our first research project to the launch of the Peatland Code, and at least five more years before the Code was making a measurable difference. In the meantime, I and many others have been working on the broader idea that ecosystem markets could significantly speed and scale-up our attempts to reach net zero in the land use sector, and we have now reached a point where this idea is an integral part of the Scottish Government's National Strategy for Economic Transformation, and the English Government is targeting a £1 billion per year market in ecosystem services. There is not a farmer in the country who is not now aware that their land could be part of the solution to climate change and that they might be able to tap into carbon markets to pay for a transition to more sustainable practices. Between the implementation of the Code and its ultimate impact, Pete and I identified multiple nodes in the system that remain to this day open to change. Depending on how this system changes in future, the outcomes we worked so hard to achieve may be under threat. A policy that is working today could yet still fail or lead to negative unintended consequences.

What had started as a failed attempt to understand the natural and social science of the complex system we were trying to influence via policy had morphed into the art of constantly adapting to changing circumstances and the opportunities and challenges that these brought. Although we wrote up our work for impact assessments in 2014 and 2021, there is no actual end point. In fact, as climate politics increasingly shift from offsetting strategies to prioritise reductions in emissions from a company's operations and decarbonising their supply chains, I am now questioning many of the assumptions behind the funding model that has enabled us to restore so many peatlands. But rather than trying to protect the legacy of our former work, the goal is to constantly adapt, to manage the negative unintended consequences arising from our work and remain relevant, even if that means starting from scratch with a new economic model. There are no rules or guidelines that can guide pivots like this, but only the values underpinning the responsible policy impact framework, which I introduced in Chapter 3: curiosity, humility, reflexivity, openness and empathy.

The outcomes I was able to describe in the systems model with Peter Barbrook-Johnson are what Peter Hall described as second-order policy change, in his 1993 article in *Comparative Politics*. Second-order shifts build on current policy and experience and can include wholesale change to existing policies and the development of new policy instruments.

However, the majority of policy changes resulting from research are first-order shifts. These are incremental changes that build on the lessons of past policy, correcting mistakes and making gradual adjustments to the overall course a policy might be taking. Only rarely are third-order shifts seen, leading to more fundamental paradigm shifts in policy, for example if the ecosystem markets we've developed were to become part of a degrowth policy agenda, channelling company profits into environmental health and wellbeing rather than the pursuit of endless growth.

Evidence suggests that between elections, policy systems are relatively stable most of the time, pursuing first-order change, based on the 'path dependency' of previous decisions and the limited attention and bandwidth that policy colleagues can give to any one issue at any time.

However, within this stability is the potential for second- and third-order shifts that can take place unexpectedly and rapidly, often in response to crises or other focusing events, which are often amplified by those seeking change, to capture the attention of decision-makers and push for change. This suggests that to affect change in a complex system, it may be better to wait for a 'policy window' of opportunity than to push an idea before anyone has sufficient interest or bandwidth. That's not to say that you can't start planning for policy impacts now, before windows open. The reason for this is that the kinds of event that create policy windows are typically urgent, requiring the development of solutions at a speed that is not suited to the typical research project. As a result, there are two ways you can prepare for a policy window.

First, to use a metaphor from biology, you need to take an evolutionary rather than a creationist approach to the development of policy options. God might have been able to create the world in seven days, but you're unlikely to be able to develop a solution to a major policy issue in a week. As a result, most policy windows are opportunities for existing ideas rather than opportunities to develop new ideas. This means that the more different policy ideas you are working on, the more likely it is that you will be able to adapt one of them for use in a policy window. In this model, the survival of the fittest ideas come down to their technical and political feasibility. Ideas for which there is already evidence have already passed the technical feasibility test. You may also have evidence of their political feasibility in terms of public acceptance or the cost of implementation. The Peatland Code was just one of a number of ideas the charity I volunteer for was working on at the time. Their initial focus had been on protecting undamaged peat bogs, but they also had been working on proposals for a ban on the use of peat in compost and a new subsidy to encourage people farming peatlands for things like carrots to switch to wetland crops for biofuels, to keep what was left of the peat from being oxidised and washed away. It took a further decade for the horticultural peat ban idea to come of age, and we're still working on the transition to wetland crops.

To understand their political feasibility, the second thing you can do to prepare for a window of opportunity is to study the policy system, with its institutions, people and teams, and the current policies in the space you're working in. It is not enough for a problem to reach the top of the political agenda and for there to be a feasible solution to the problem. Decision-makers need a motive to turn your solution into policy. Such motives can be opaque, but with sufficient study, it is often possible to find a personal, constituency or some other special interest of a minister or to link your solution to existing national or international policy targets or commitments to motivate civil servants to act.

When we first pitched the idea of peatland carbon markets, we were working with a labour-led government that took both conservation and climate change seriously, so they were instantly attracted to the biodiversity and climate benefits of restoring peatlands. Next however, we were working under a coalition government with a Conservative minister who wasn't interested in conservation and was a climate denier. Our pitch to him still pointed out the biodiversity and climate benefits of our proposal, but consistent with his conservative values, we emphasised the role of the market and how this could reduce reliance on public budgets. This got our idea into a government White Paper, but then things stalled. The next minister had other priorities and wasn't pushing forward the proposals of his predecessor, wanting instead to create his own legacy. Like many of his conservative colleagues at the time, he was pushing for Brexit, and happened to like walking in the hills of his constituency, where he had come to realise that hill farmers might be among the worst hit by Brexit. Again, we pointed out that our goals as a conservation charity were biodiversity and climate, but we also pointed out that our policy instrument could potentially put more money in the pockets of hill farmers than the European Union could through our current subsidy system. Instantly, he was on side.

The last minister we tried to reach prior to the launch of the Code never met conservation charities on principle. He turned out to be completely unreachable. So, the director of our charity at the time took an unexpected step and invited a policy consultant (aka. lobbyist) to our offices. I remember watching him open a little black book in which he showed us his contacts with various members of the royal family, lords and ladies, CEOs of major companies and famous actors (including Benedict Cumberbatch). For his half-price charity rate of £500 per day, he told us he would introduce us to his friends. By the time I had heard his plan, I was very glad it was our director, not me who would have to do the meeting and greeting. The result was a series of dinner parties hosted by conservative Lords in country estates with grouse shooting on peatlands. By the third dinner party, enough of them were convinced that it was a good idea, and when the current minister just happened to be there on a shooting trip, his friends ended up pitched our proposal to him, and he thought it a grand idea.

PROTECTING GAINS IN COMPLEX SYSTEM

Once decisions have been made, to protect the gains achieved by the new policy, a degree of stability is needed. Although elections can be a major risk, I've shown how we kept reframing our policy to meet the ideologies and political needs of successive ministers in different administrations. Although some might see this as manipulative, I would argue that this was a legitimate influencing process because it was transparent (we never hid the fact that we were doing it for the environment) and for the public good (in addition to biodiversity and climate benefits, fixing damaged peatlands can improve water quality and reduce flood risk). However, we are not complacent about the gains we have made. As my work with Pete Barbrook-Johnson showed, there are a number of volatile components of the system that has generated the current outcomes, and each of these need to be managed. But not at any cost. One of the potential sources of volatility is a change in the scientific consensus about the benefits of peatland restoration. If this were to shift, suggesting that the work we are doing is in fact causing more harm than good, then we would need to pivot from a strategy of policy implementation to damage limitation, trying to undo or avoid any further harms.

One of the challenges of maintaining stability around policies that work is that there may be others seeking to disrupt that stability and reverse the policies you have striven to support. Depending on where your research sits in relation to policies that are currently stable and unquestioned, you may want to become the disruptor. Most people start by critiquing the current policy, but depending on the level of investment in the current policy, the politically feasible options for change may be heavily constrained (the idea of path dependency mentioned earlier). As a result, the next strategy is known as 'venue shopping', where you seek out others within government, the civil service, the opposition or wider policy networks who might support the change you are seeking. For example:

- Is there a credible 'government in waiting' in opposition that might come to power at the next election? If so, there is a strong possibility that they are looking for new, disruptive policy ideas for inclusion in their manifesto.
- Look for another comparable country that might be more receptive to your ideas, and work with them instead, refining your approach and gathering evidence of what works, ready to take your idea back to your own country when a policy window appears (such as a new minister or government). This is easy enough in the UK, where right-wing parties have tended to rule England while more socialist parties have tended to rule Wales and Scotland. Otherwise, start with other countries that have similar political systems and are similar enough in relation to the issues you're working on (e.g. we have exported the Peatland Code as a model to a number of other countries with significant greenhouse gas emissions from their peatlands).
- Join or form a coalition with others who share your interests and are interested in your ideas. You can do this systematically using the methods in Chapter 5. Together you can use these methods to build an impact strategy in which you will be able to share the work of achieving change with many others. This is why I started working for the peatland charity. It was clear to me that I didn't have the time, expertise or connections to pursue the idea for a Peatland Code that had emerged from our research project. However, the idea helped further the goals of the charity, which had the time, expertise and connections that I didn't have. Together, we were able to achieve things that would not have been possible apart.

If we view policy as a complex system, then we need to rethink our role as researchers. We can never know enough to make any kind of policy recommendation with any real certainty. That means that our role doesn't stop once we've delivered our evidence to the decision-makers. Instead, we need to stay with the policy process, helping trouble-shoot and adapt, drawing on evidence wherever possible and, where there is no evidence, informing debate and helping guide our policy colleagues as best we can as we all try our best to adapt to limitations and circumstance. This more evolutionary approach to policy sees our work as part of a joint, ongoing experiment with our policy colleagues. Our role is not to predict the outcome but to use whatever evidence we have, to help evaluate options and help our policy colleagues adapt the implementation of these policies as they unfold. Rather than aiming for the big third-order changes, we should probably be more realistic and make ourselves useful with first-order tweaks as we develop multiple ideas that could deliver more significant (second-order) change, as the opportunity arises. Much of the complexity in policy systems arises from the people who inhabit them and their different and shifting priorities, power and strategies. Understanding who is most relevant to engage with and how to engage effectively in policy networks, when you have limited time, is therefore the focus of Chapter 5.

CHAPTER 5

Navigating relationships

As I have shown in Chapter 4, we are not working with policy in a vacuum. In addition to our policy colleagues, we need to also pay attention to the many other people and organisations in wider policy networks, who come in and out of influence as their interests intersect with current policy agendas. More importantly however, the people (and non-human species) and issues we are seeking to help are largely overlooked in policy impact guides and toolkits.

Failure to engage with these groups can be a major barrier to impact, leading to the generation of unintended consequences for those who were not engaged, whose knowledge and perspectives were not considered. You may inadvertently inflame conflicts, resulting in alienation and distrust, or enable powerful groups to dominate decision-making, marginalising other groups and voices and potentially biasing outcomes. This is particularly problematic when these groups are already marginalised, further delegitimising their knowledge and alienating vulnerable people.

The more effort you invest in representing different voices in your policy work, the more potential you have to amplify diverse voices, generating more realistic assessments of policy problems and more creative and appropriate solutions. I will consider how to manage power and privilege in these processes in greater depth in Chapter 6. Here, I want to focus on the tools and skills you need to identify and form working relationships with policy colleagues, organisations in policy networks and the people who are meant to benefit from public policy.

WHO IS MOST RELEVANT TO ENGAGE WITH?

I am starting with the assumption that you have a good knowledge of your research area and the policy landscape linked to the issues you study. If not, then you will need to have a basic appreciation of the key

DOI: 10.4324/9781003494942-6

policies, political agendas, departments, agencies and key influencers in your research field. It may be useful to find a colleague who can mentor you and, as you consider options, ask if there might be someone in your network who is outside academia who might be able to help (your social media network might be one place to start looking). You might want to use the tool I will describe in this section, in a session with your mentor, to start exploring their knowledge of the policy landscape in your research area.

Assuming you understand the key issues of the day as they relate to your research expertise, then the first step in any attempt to engage with policy is to identify everyone who may be interested in, have the power to influence or be affected by these issues. If you work across very different issues, then you might want to go through this process for one issue at a time. At this point, you only need to have a basic understanding of the key issues and policies relating to your field of work. You will do a more detailed assessment of the evidence needs and policy gaps once you have identified the right people to speak to. In this way, you will be sure that the gaps and needs you identify are real, felt needs and important gaps that need attention, rather than attempting to work this out from your 'ivory tower'.

Traditionally, 'stakeholder analysis' is used as a tool to identify and prioritise who you should engage with. However, in my latest research in this field, I am highly critical of their simplistic focus on those who have the most interest and influence. These were described as the 'key players' in the literature that originally proposed the approach, encouraging users of the tool to exclude those with limited interest or power (who they tellingly called 'the crowd'), to more efficiently focus on those most likely to be able to affect change. But what if the groups in society who will be most affected by the policies you are working on have no power and are too busy surviving to be interested in your work? As a result, the uncritical use of these tools has systematically marginalised some of the most vulnerable groups that should have been prioritised for engagement.

To add insult to injury, concerns have also been raised with the word 'stakeholder' itself. I recently published a paper arguing that the word should no longer be used, as part of a wider effort to decolonise research vocabulary. Partly this relates to its use in colonial history, for example by settlers in what is now Canada, who 'staked' out their claim to the land prior to any treaty with First Nations groups. Although it is possible to argue that there are other older histories to this word, it is impossible to escape the Western ways of knowing and being that it expresses. We stake out, mark as our own and keep others out – and increasingly, that's the sort of behaviour we see as researchers compete to build exclusive relationships with policy teams that could give them high-value impacts. However, this stands at odds with non-Western ways of knowing and being, expressed powerfully in this poem by Josie Valadez Fraire, an indigenous woman writer born on occupied Cheyenne, Arapaho, and Ute territory in what is now Boulder, Colorado (reproduced here with her permission):

> Colonised minds
> hear
> "ours"
> and think of
> possession.
>
> Decolonising minds
> hear
> "ours"
> and feel
> connection.

For this reason, as you will have seen already, I use a range of different words, depending on exactly who I am talking about, including people, groups, colleagues, partners and non-human species, and in my academic work, I often use the term 'relevant parties', drawing on Edward Freeman's original 1984 original definition of stakeholders as 'groups and individuals who can affect, or are affected by' an action or decision (p. 52).

To try and think more critically about these issues, I have proposed a third criterion that we can use to identify and prioritise who we should engage with: impact. One of the reasons I chose this as the criterion is that impacts can be positive or negative, and it is just as important to understand how a policy will benefit as it will harm or disadvantage a particular group. It also helpfully begins with the same letter as the existing two criteria, interest and influence, so I call this a 3i analysis, instead of a stakeholder analysis. By including impact, the goal is to ensure that disempowered groups are not further marginalised, while identifying benefits that could be delivered and mitigating the risk that they experience negative unintended consequences. In summary, to do this analysis, you need to ask three questions:

1. Who is interested (or not)?
2. Who has influence (to facilitate or block impact) or is voiceless, power-less, marginalised and/or hard-to-reach?
3. Who might be directly impacted (positively or negatively)?

Table 5.1 shows how the analysis seeks to understand interest, influence and impact at a primary and a secondary, deeper level. By considering these two levels, you will be able to build up a more comprehensive understanding of who is most relevant to engage with than is possible with a traditional stakeholder analysis, uncovering hidden dynamics that might be driving interactions and outcomes. The primary level of analysis seeks to provide the kind of shallow but useful initial assessment of who might be relevant that you would see in a traditional stakeholder analysis, considering each group's stated interests and preferences and their explicit, hierarchical 'power over' influence. These kinds of influence are typically characterised by control, instrumentalism and self-interest and driven by factors such as access to resources, organisational scale, property rights and levels of authority and expertise. In addition, you will consider the short-term benefits or negative impacts arising from initial engagement with each group, for example as part of a research project or during policy development. This may include, for example, the formation of new networks, capacity, knowledge or skills and the possible risks that may arise, such as inflaming conflict or misunderstandings that could lead to disengagement.

Table 5.1 The two levels for clarifying interest, influence and impact.

	Interest	Influence	Impact
Primary	Stated interest and preferences	Explicit, hierarchical 'power over'	Immediate benefits or negative impacts from initial engagement
Secondary	Underpinning (transcendental) values beliefs and norms	Implicit, personal and transpersonal 'power with'	Longer term benefits or negative impacts

The secondary level of analysis aims to provide additional insights that might enable you to engage more empathically and effectively with each of the groups you have identified. It does this by questioning assumptions and facilitating deeper discussions about the values, beliefs and norms that shape people's stated interests and preferences and more implicit, personal and transpersonal 'power with' influence. This kind of influence is typically characterised by dialogue, inclusion, networks, negotiation and shared power. For example, a landlord has 'power over' their tenant farmer due to the legally binding restrictions contained within a tenancy agreement, whereas a farmers' union, which tries to guide or influence tenant farmers towards, say, adopting certain environmental practices, has 'power with' its members. In both cases, influence can act to facilitate or block change. In addition to short-term impacts, the second level of analysis also considers the longer term benefits or negative impacts likely to accrue to each group as a policy is implemented in the real world. This could include instrumental benefits, such as new policies, or economic, social, environmental, health or cultural benefits arising from the issue, intervention, project, process or decision as it plays out, or negative impacts that might arise as an unintended consequence.

In Table 5.2, I have designed a series of questions to facilitate discussion (where the analysis is conducted via a workshop) or feed into a survey (where this method is preferred to conduct the analysis) at both the

Table 5.2 Questions to identify relevant parties for engagement based on the dimensions of interest, influence and impact, including questions to facilitate analysis at both the primary and secondary levels described in Table 5.1.

Dimension of the analysis	Primary-level questions	Secondary-level questions
Interest	Which parties are already interested and what is the nature of their interest? • What is the scope of their interest? • What aspects of an issue are they interested in? • Who within the group or which part of the organisation is most interested? Who else would you like do you think should be interested? • Why should they be interested?	• What values, beliefs, norms or assumptions might be influencing their *perception* of the issue, intervention, project, process or decision? • What values, beliefs, norms or assumptions might be driving or inhibiting the *interest or disinterest* in the issue, intervention, project, process or decision?

(Continued)

Table 5.2 Questions to identify relevant parties for engagement based on the dimensions of interest, influence and impact, including questions to facilitate analysis at both the primary and secondary levels described in Table 5.1. *(Continued)*

Dimension of the analysis	Primary-level questions	Secondary-level questions
Influence	Which parties have the power to *facilitate* development of positive or negative impacts in relation to this issue, intervention, project, process or decision? • Do they have direct influence over impacts, for example via access to resources, organisational scale, property rights or levels of authority and expertise that give them 'power over' others? • Which individuals with a group or groups within an organisation have most influence to facilitate impact and why? Who has the power to *block* development of these impacts? • Do they have direct influence over impacts? • Which individuals or groups have most influence to block impact and why? Who or what can they influence and at what geographical, social or other scale?	• Who has indirect influence to facilitate or block impacts, for example via dialogue, inclusion, networks, negotiation and shared power that give them 'power with' others? • Which individuals or groups within organisations have most influence to facilitate or block impact in these ways? • Who or what can they influence and at what geographical, social or other scale?
Impact	Which parties might benefit most in the short term from initial engagement with this issue, intervention, project, process or decision? • What types of benefits are likely to be gained for each of these parties, for example the formation of new networks, capacity, knowledge or skills? Which parties may be disadvantaged or harmed most in the short term, from initial engagement with this issue, intervention, project, process or decision? • What risks are these parties likely to be exposed to or disadvantages might they suffer, such as inflaming conflict or misunderstandings that could lead to disengagement?	Which parties might benefit most in the long term as a result of the issue, intervention, project, process or decision as it plays out? • What types of benefits are likely to be gained for each of these parties, for example new policies or economic, social, environmental, health or cultural benefits? • How significant and far-reaching are these impacts anticipated to be? Which parties may be disadvantaged or harmed most in the long term, as this issue, intervention, project, process or decision plays out? • What risks are these parties likely to be exposed to or disadvantages might they suffer, for example as a result of negative unintended consequences? • How significant and far-reaching are these impacts anticipated to be?

primary and secondary levels described in Table 5.1. Questions are posed in both positive and negative forms to capture those with and without interest and influence those who may be negatively or positively impacted by the issue, intervention, project, process or decision. Table 5.3 provides a table that can be used to capture answers to these questions individually or in workshops.

To illustrate what this analysis might look like, Figure 5.1 summarises a 3i analysis I did recently, showing the range of different types of organisations identified, and Table 5.4 summarises what I learned from this analysis about the policy organisations working on this particular issue (ecosystem markets). As you can see, in addition to providing an overview of the complex network of organisations and groups engaging on this issue, it provides a deep level of understanding of each group's interest and influence and the likely impact these markets might have for them.

To illustrate the different forms of power that you might have to work with, and what can go wrong when you don't assess interest, influence and impact systematically, I would like to take you back to one of my first experiences of working with policy as an Early Career Researcher (ECR). We had been funded by a research funder and government as part of a United Nations (UN) initiative to create a 'national ecosystem assessment'. While we were setting up the project, one of my colleagues was approached by an environmental charity who wanted us to extend our work by collecting some additional data. Without consulting the existing funders, I accepted the additional funding for the extra work. When we had finished the research, the charity was delighted with the findings from the work they had commissioned. As they had expected, our research showed that the marine strategy being developed by the Government was fundamentally flawed. Their CEO phoned me immediately, saying she wanted to go to the media with the findings, to try and force a policy U-turn. I had briefed my policy colleagues at the same time, and they were instantly concerned about the political fall-out from our research. Moreover, they were unhappy about that lack of control they had over the timing and nature of any publicity around our work, given that I had already told the charity what we'd found. Government-funded research that proves the Government wrong is clearly a political problem, if handled badly.

Table 5.3 The 3i analytical framework

Name of organisation, group or individual	Interest				Influence (indirect)
Relevant Party 1 (named)	**Scope of interest:** geographical or other relevant scope (Closed answer question: regional, national, or multi-national)	**Nature of interest (preferences):** which parties are *already* interested and what is the nature of their interest? Who do you think should be interested? (describe)	**Nature of interest (values):** what values, beliefs, norms or assumptions might be influencing their perception of or interest/disinterest in the issue, intervention, project, process or decision? (describe)	**Level of interest** in the work (Closed answer question: high, medium, or low)	**Nature of influence (direct power over):** which parties have direct influence or 'power over' others to facilitate or block development of positive or negative impacts? Are there individuals or groups within organisations with more influence? (describe)

I had planned to visit London later that week, so I asked the charity if they could wait until I had discussed the findings properly with the policy team, which she was happy to do, on the understanding that if I couldn't convince the government to change its plans, she reserved the right to go to the media. By the time I reached Whitehall, my civil servant colleague had hatched a plan. The minister, he told me, was politically committed to announcing the new strategy at an event the following week. Everyone knew what the government was planning (hence our commission), so changing tack publicly at an event like this would leave the politician red-faced. However, he had been briefed on our evidence and knew that his strategy wouldn't work. He would therefore announce his strategy as a 'direction of travel' rather than a firm policy commitment. And then, he would quietly U-turn his strategy to align with the evidence after the glare of the cameras had moved on, avoiding political embarrassment. He followed through on this

	Impact (direct)					Other context
Nature of influence (indirect power with): which parties have indirect influence or 'power with' others to facilitate or block development of positive or negative impacts? Are there individuals or groups within organisations with more influence? (describe)	**Reach of influence:** who or what can they influence and at what geographical, social or other scale? (describe)	**Level of influence:** in the research (high/ medium/ low)	**Nature of impact (short term):** which parties might benefit or be disadvantaged most in the short term from initial engagement with this issue, intervention, project, process or decision? (describe)	**Nature of impact (long term):** which parties might benefit or be disadvantaged most in the long term as a result of the issue, intervention, project, process or decision as it plays out? (describe)	**Level of impact:** how significant and far-reaching are the identified impacts likely to be? (Closed answer question: high, medium or low)	For example: knowledge base, expertise, funding and political context (describe)

promise, and ultimately everyone was happy with the outcome. But I very quickly realised that I had been used as a political pawn in a much longer game that had been played by the environmental charity, who, despite their limited size and funding, had used our evidence and the threat of media coverage to achieve their policy goal. I went into this situation blind because I hadn't done any systematic analysis of the organisations involved or taken the time to sit down properly with the two key players to understand their antagonistic history and opposing plans for our research.

MAKING CONNECTIONS

Once you have identified the relevant organisations and groups in this way, the next step is to make contact, so you can explore their needs in greater depth, start building relationships and consider the sorts of alliances and

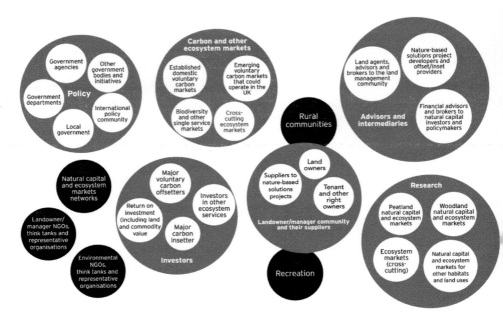

Figure 5.1 Organisations and groups with interest or influence or likely to be impacted by the development of high-integrity ecosystem markets.

other strategies you might want to build to affect policy change. There is no single way of doing this, but you might want to consider prioritising those who will be particularly impacted but who have limited interest or influence, as these groups will often be vulnerable or challenging to engage and reaching out to these groups may take considerable thought and effort. You will also want to prioritise those who are highly interested, influential and impacted, as they will be likely to want to engage and may join forces with you to collaborate on your policy engagement.

These often include government bodies and influential third-sector organisations working on the issues you are interested in. It was just such an analysis, many years ago, which led me to the charity I now volunteer for. I was doing the analysis as part of a research project and so was able to work with a social network analysis to do a more granular analysis than is strictly necessary (the methods I've proposed above will get you to the same place much more quickly and easily). Figure 5.2 shows our analysis of this particular policy network. The size of organisational nodes is proportional to their importance in terms of the amount of information they received on the policy issue we were studying

Table 5.4 Categories and sub-categories of organisations and groups emerging from a 3i analysis of UK ecosystem markets.

Policy

Category	Description	Examples	Interest	Influence	Impact
Government departments and teams	Teams and groups within government responsible for aspects of natural capital and ecosystem markets policy and regulation	• Department for Environment, Food and Rural Affairs (Defra) • Environment and Forestry Directorate (Scottish Government) • Department of Agriculture, Environment and Rural Affairs (Northern Ireland Executive) • Joint Nature Conservation Committee	Interested in ensuring high-integrity markets supplement public funding for climate and nature recovery while generating wider public benefits and avoiding negative unintended consequences. This interest assumes there is insufficient public funding to reach a nature-positive net zero, which has been questioned by some as a policy decision to deprioritise the environment. More socialist administrations are more sceptical and risk-averse around engaging with private finance.	Each department has jurisdictional influence over policy in only one UK country as ecosystem markets (other than the UK Emissions Trading Scheme) are devolved. Civil service teams working on these issues are typically small, under-funded and part of departments concerned with agriculture that need to keep the farming community 'on side', limiting the influence of these teams internally.	Ecosystem markets have the potential to impact the ability of each administration to reach net zero and nature recovery targets for the land use sector by substantially supplementing the public funding that is currently available. These administrations also have responsibility for rural communities and tenant farmers who stand to lose much from these markets, and their needs must be balanced with the need to reach targets.
Government agencies	Government agencies and other bodies with statutory powers responsible for natural capital policy implementation	• NatureScot, Natural England and Natural Resources Wales • National Park Authorities • Scottish Forestry, Forestry & Land Scotland and Forestry England	Each has a more sectoral or location-specific context in which they are likely to engage with high-integrity markets, facilitating their operation through their land and functions.	Agencies are primarily responsible for implementing policy, but experts from these organisations are regularly engaged in policy development and can help ensure ecosystem market policies are likely to work on the ground. Their powers of enforcement give them 'power over' rather than 'power with' landowners who often dislike these bodies	These agencies are typically under-funded and under significant pressure to deliver policy targets. Additional resources from ecosystem markets could make it easier to meet some targets, delivering climate change mitigation alongside biodiversity uplift.

(Continued)

Table 5.4 Categories and sub-categories of organisations and groups emerging from a 3i analysis of UK ecosystem markets. *(Continued)*

Category	Description	Examples	Interest	Influence	Impact
Local government	Local councils and planning authorities with interests in natural capital	• Local Planning Authorities and Forestry Commission offices • Local Councils with interests in natural capital • Local Government Association, Convention of Scottish Local Authorities	Interested in harnessing high-integrity ecosystem markets to deliver nature-based solutions that provide wider benefits to the communities in their area.	Planning and forestry authorities have significant power to require developers to fund nature restoration projects to offset biodiversity impacts and to approve or amend planned forestry developments.	Local government bodies are typically under-funded and ecosystem markets could provide much-needed funding, for example to pay for natural flood management schemes to protect local communities.
Other government bodies and initiatives	A range of other cross-UK bodies and Scottish and UK policy initiatives are working on natural capital and ecosystem markets	• UK Ecosystem Markets Policy Coordination Group (connecting Scottish Government, Defra, Welsh and Northern Irish policy teams) • Committee on Climate Change (CCC) • Scottish Enterprise and Social Enterprise UK • Just Transition Commission	Interested in learning from different UK jurisdictions and where possible harmonising policy and governance to avoid market distortions across borders.	Most of these bodies and initiatives can advise but not dictate policy. The CCC's role overseeing legally binding climate targets gives it more power than most similar bodies to hold governments to account across the UK.	By sharing knowledge and expertise, networks like the policy coordination group can save policy officers time and enable them to perform better by avoiding duplication and implementing lessons from and collaborations with colleagues in other UK countries. Groups like the Just Transition Commission consult with and give voice to those most likely to be disadvantaged by ecosystem markets.

(Continued)

Table 5.4 Categories and sub-categories of organisations and groups emerging from a 3i analysis of UK ecosystem markets. *(Continued)*

Category	Description	Examples	Interest	Influence	Impact
International policy community	International organisations and task forces that either engage with or shape policy and ecosystem markets	• Task Force on Nature-Related Financial Disclosures • The Global Ethical Finance Initiative • The International Council for Voluntary Carbon Markets, Voluntary Carbon Markets Integrity Initiative	Interested in increasing the integrity of ecosystem markets internationally, with a strong focus on international voluntary carbon markets.	None of these bodies have the power to get their guidance adopted or implemented by nation states but, by working with industry, are putting pressure on governments to adopt harmonised standards, to ensure the effective operation of global markets.	If adopted widely, these initiatives have the potential to become self-sustaining and grow in influence internationally, helping to boost confidence in ecosystem markets, driving investment and climate change mitigation.

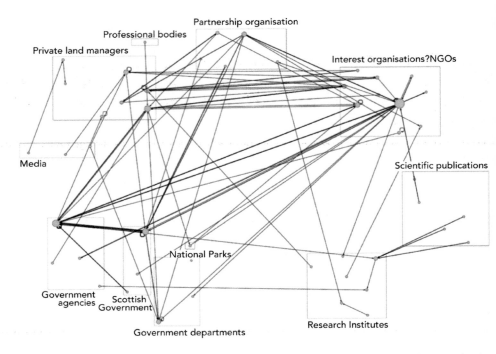

Figure 5.2 Social network showing the pathways of information flow related to research on peatlands and climate change in a Scottish policy network. Each node represents an organisation, and the ties between nodes show the sum of information exchanges about specific research findings as reported by individual respondents. Organisations are grouped by type shown by the labelling of the boxes. The size of the node shows its degree of centrality (the number of links the node – organisation – has). The arrow heads show the direction of the information pathway. The network is based on data from individuals in the following groups: the Scottish Government (n = 5), interest organisations/NGOs (n = 11), government agencies (n = 7) and research institutes (n = 6).

from different organisations in their network. The thickness of the lines shows the amount of information they passed to others in the network, with thick lines representing significant information flows. It shows that a non-governmental organisation (see the top right of Figure 5.2 in the centre of the interest organisations/NGOs cluster) was one of the most influential organisations in the network, and as such, it became one of the first organisations I reached out to. Little did I know at the time that I would end up actually volunteering for them.

Once you have completed your analysis, you will want to identify the relevant teams within these organisations and key contacts from those teams who you can reach out to, to start building connections. There are three ways of doing this. First, go to your professional networks to see if your colleagues already are already connected to the organisations you have identified. You could do this within your institution, your disciplinary networks or via contacts on social media. This is my preferred options, wherever possible, because you are more likely to get a reply and be able to set up a meeting if you are introduced by someone who is already trusted.

Second, search online and via social media. Many organisations publish organograms and have named team members with biographies that you can use to identify the most relevant person to reach out to. Failing this, social media can be a powerful tool for both identifying and contacting relevant people. LinkedIn, in particular, has a particularly powerful search function, if you have enough relevant connections on the platform. If you are not using the platform or have a very small network of your own, consider approaching colleagues with relevant LinkedIn networks to ask them to perform a search. A colleague recently asked me if I knew anyone who worked on climate change in a particular government department (he was following my first connecting strategy above). I told him that I didn't know anyone, but I would have a look on LinkedIn. There were four people in my LinkedIn network working in that department, but when I widened the search to second- and third-degree connections (colleagues of colleagues of these four people), it came up with a list of over 600 people working on climate change. I sent the person the names and job titles of a few who looked most relevant, and they were able to find their email addresses online and make contact.

Finally, if all else fails, you may consider hiring a company that specialises in public affairs, public relations or strategic communication – all euphemisms for lobbying. Although I felt uneasy working with the gentleman I referred to in Chapter 4 with his little black book of contacts, not everyone does. I know of one university whose Vice Chancellor who is open about his use of a strategic communications company staffed by ex-civil servants to get access to high-level decision-makers within government. UK Research and Innovation, the main funder of research in the UK, has a section on getting support from 'specialist agencies' like this in the section of their *Impact Toolkit* on *How to influence policymakers*. However, the eye-watering fees these companies charge for the advice that accompanies their introductions means that this strategy is out of reach for most researchers and members of the public, and it is this idea that only the rich can use these agencies to get privileged access to politicians that worries me. If we are using these privileges to do good, does the end justify the means? Personally, I think not, but I will let you judge for yourself.

BUILDING CONNECTION

Now that you have identified a small group of the most important people you want to reach out to first, you need to set up meetings with each organisation. By referring to your 3i analysis, you will be able to appreciate the different interests of each organisation and can write a tailored message to each, based on the intersection of your interests. To one, you might emphasise the potential of your research to address a challenge that you think is particularly felt by that group. To another, you might explain how your research might help them meet a strategic goal, based on what you've learned about their organisation. As a result, you are much more likely to get a positive response, compared to sending out the same invitation to everyone.

Once you get a meeting with someone, it is essential that you fight any urge you might have to prove yourself or share everything you know. Instead, you need to ground yourself in the principles I described in Chapter 3:

- The first of these was curiosity, which is a super-power for most researchers. Your task is to turn to the person in front of you with the same curiosity that draws you into your research, cultivating curiosity as a skill by asking probing questions, including at least some starting with the word 'why'.
- You may have world-leading expertise in your subject area, but the person sitting in front of you has expertise you do not possess related to the policies you want to influence. It is essential that you learn from them, but to do so requires the humility to acknowledge the limitations of your own knowledge and question what you thought you already knew.
- We need to be aware of the invisible power dynamics that may influence how we are coming across to the other person, based on the privilege and power we hold as researchers.

NAVIGATING RELATIONSHIPS **61**

- We need to be open to perspectives that differ from our own, asking why the other person has reached such different conclusions rather than seeking to prove them wrong. The more open we are about our own values and biases, the less is hidden and the more trustworthy we will become.

By enacting each of these principles, we increase the likelihood of empathic connection, the last of the five principles I introduced earlier. Given that the people you are interacting with may have wildly different values and attitudes to you, some of which may offend you, your task is to avoid falling prey to what many psychologists have called 'empathy bias'. We are instinctively less likely to reach out to or establish empathic connection with people who are very different to us. The bigger the difference is, the harder it is to establish connection. And yet as human beings, we all have something in common. That's why when I am meeting policy colleagues in person, I like to invite them for tea or coffee, and instantly, we find something not connected to work to chat about while we wait our turn to be served. When meeting people online, I always start asking them what sort of week they are having, or if it is a Monday how they enjoyed their weekend, to try and start with a conversation that has a chance of finding some kind of human connection before moving to work chat. When I am training researchers in networking skills online, I start by putting everyone into paired breakout rooms and invite them to choose an object from their desk or office to show to their partner and to use the object to tell a short story that says something about them. They take turns, and in less than five minutes, everyone has found out at least one thing about their colleague that they didn't know before, and they are usually curious to find out more. When I invite them to reflect on the exercise, most people can usually infer many things about their partner's priorities and values, based on this small window into their lives. We are all more than our job; real networks are based on empathic connection.

After a few meetings like this, you will have a stronger sense of the people and the pressures they are under, as well as the issues, evidence gaps and policy needs they are grappling with. As a result, you will be in a much stronger position to make a strategic plan for influencing policy that takes into account these challenges and limitations. If you have built a strong connection, you may even be able to persuade some of the people you have met to help you co-create this, linking to their own plans for policy impact. In other cases, where there are already well-developed plans, your task is to work out how you can add value to existing work rather than develop your own master plan. I will discuss this further in Chapter 6.

Before that though, I want to conclude this chapter by thinking about how you can build on these initial connections to make strong and lasting networks. Despite trying to develop methods for prioritising who is relevant that avoid marginalising vulnerable groups, I still often feel uneasy about the Machiavellian ways these analyses can be used. When we strategically target people for a purpose (in this case, policy impact), people can end up feeling used. Just think about how you felt the last time you were targeted by a salesperson trying to get a sale. There is a sense that the person you are talking is feigning interest in you, but in reality they are only interested in their purpose, which usually serves them more than it serves you. Similarly, your policy colleagues are likely to view you as an impact salesperson if all you want to do is sell your latest research in return for some impact. They need to know that you are actually reaching out to them because you share their passion, genuinely want to help (whether or not it will further your impact) and are curious to get to know them as a person. To paraphrase the slogan about getting pets for Christmas: networks are for life, not just for impact.

DEEPENING YOUR NETWORKS

The primary goal of networking then is connection, with impact a secondary consideration. If you are successful, you will connect deeply enough to see the world through the eyes of the people you want to help, and as a result, you see things differently. You will be able to learn from multiple perspectives and create new opportunities between people who you can see have something to gain from connecting with each other.

Connection is the reason that policy networking can come as naturally to introverts as it does to extroverts. While having lots of contacts can be useful sometimes, the quality of your relationships matters more than the number of people in your address book when you actually need help with something. If you need anything that requires more than a couple of minutes of someone's attention, you're unlikely to get anything meaningful back by crowdsourcing on social media. You need to go to people with whom you have social capital.

When I left Newcastle University, I needed to find someone who might stand in for me as lead supervisor for one of my PhD students, doing the paperwork while letting me continue to operate (effectively) as lead supervisor from my new institution so that the student would experience minimal disruption. I needed someone who was both willing to do me a favour with the paperwork and who would trust that I would continue to play the lead supervisor role despite getting no credit for this work at my new institution. Rather than putting out a social media message or contacting the research group, I went straight to the one person who knew me best and who I had bent over backwards to help whenever they'd asked me in the past: my line manager. We both trusted each other enough to know we could make it work, and all I needed was one person. Connection starts with a single person.

You already have your 3i analysis to guide you to the right teams in the most relevant organisations, but the number of people you could potentially reach out to can be overwhelming. It isn't uncommon for me to identify over 100 organisations in a 3i analysis, and I don't have time to reach out to even a fraction of them, let alone build relationships with them. As a result, I take a nested approach to my relationship building. I may regularly connect on a superficial level with two or three key organisations in each category of my analysis, resulting in electronic communication with 10-15 people from different organisations in the course of a typical month. But within each main categories, there is a small number of people who I make sure I am in close contact with. I do everything possible to make time for them and help them whenever they ask. One of them got in touch today – he's a 'VIP' on my phone so I couldn't miss the notification of his email, and he wanted to talk urgently about an opportunity. My diary is currently full for the rest of the month, but I have a writing day tomorrow that I've diligently protected from diary appointments. However, despite saying 'no' to countless meetings and invitations to protect that writing time, I told him to ring my mobile whenever he gets a chance so we can chat through his opportunity. The problem is that this is time-consuming and so you can only ever do this for a small number of people.

To give you a flavour of some of the people I regularly connect with and try my best to add value to, these include the following:

- Someone who leads a team in Scottish Government on natural capital policy;
- Someone who heads up a team working on natural capital policy in English Government;
- Someone in charge of a UN programme on peatlands, who is influencing global policy agendas, and through the UN has the capacity to inform and help shape peatland policies in countries around the world;
- Someone in charge of sustainability for a large multi-national company, who is well connected across the business and policy worlds, and helping lead the corporate sustainability agenda;
- The small team in the charity I volunteer for who are well connected across the third sector and peatland policy worlds; and
- The General Manager of the community organisation I volunteer for locally who is well connected across Scottish community organisations.

Taken together, by investing in these relationships, I'm able to add value to people who I have grown to deeply respect and care for, who have the capacity to have impact across the policy, third sector, business and community sectors in Scotland, England and internationally. This isn't to say that I won't help others, but I only have limited time, and I can't proactively reach out to add value to everyone who might benefit from my help, so I have focused my limited time and energy where I feel I can make most of a difference.

Each of these people is what's known as 'bonding' connections. Although they are seemingly very different to each other, and to me, each of these individuals shares a passion for the environment and wants to tackle the climate emergency using the best available evidence. Most researchers have bonding connections with other researchers in their disciplinary or institutional networks; it is easy to work with people who see the world in fundamentally similar ways to you. Bonding connections are typically with like-minded people. Because these people are like you, it is easy for them to empathise with you when you are in need, and as a result, networks of people with bonding connections often have a high degree of reciprocity.

However, if you want to make a difference, there are two other types of connection that you need to cultivate.

'Bridging' connections occur when you cultivate relationships with people who are very different to you. Typically, people think about the ability to create bridges of trust between different worlds, and for most researchers, building relationships with people outside academia is how you will create bridging connection. But it can go much deeper than just creating bridges between the worlds of scholars and charities, or science and policy. The hardest and most rewarding bridges are those we build to people who are fundamentally different, even objectionable, to us. Learning how to trust and be trustworthy with people who we instinctively distrust requires advanced empathy skills. This is not just being friendly to people to build social capital that you can 'cash in' at a later date, while criticising them behind their backs. This is understanding and respecting people enough that you speak well of them behind their backs, even when you know others will judge you.

I work on highly contested issues and have sought to build bridges of trust with people on each side of the debates I research. In conservation, my home discipline, it isn't always 'cool' to work with companies like Nestle or Diageo, or protect the interests of farmers, given the impact each of these groups has had on the environment. But while it is easy to demonise a company or group, it is much harder to think badly of an actual farmer who is telling you everything they are doing to nurture nature on their farm or a sustainability officer who wants to transform a company's supply chains to protect and restore nature. When you connect with these people's passion and see their heart, you can't help but build bridges of trust, even if you disagree with some of their beliefs and practices. Once you get to a person's values, it is difficult not to find something that resonates with you.

Finally, to achieve impact, researchers have a unique responsibility to foster 'bracing' connections between different hierarchical levels within their networks. This might include, for example, facilitating a connection between a farmer who has a great idea and a policymaker who might be able to act on that idea. However, it can be a challenge to create trusting relationships with people who occupy different hierarchical levels to you. If they are above you in the hierarchy, you may be invisible to them, and if they are below you, they may instinctively distrust you as one of the 'elite' who is probably 'out of touch' with people like them.

The lessons you learn from people in different disciplines and worlds, and at different places in hierarchies, can bring you insights that are very different to the kinds of ideas you get from spending time with your bonding connections, who are similar to you. Chris Argyris and Donald Schon, in their 1974 book *Theory in Practice*, described this as 'triple-loop' learning, where you are forced to re-evaluate your assumptions, values and beliefs and find new ways of learning, as opposed to the cognitive understanding of single-loop learning or the critical thinking of double-loop learning. Some of the people who have most deeply challenged how I think about and do research have been researchers from developing countries or Western development studies researchers who taught me to see my own prejudices and assumptions and those of the Western knowledge systems I was embedded in. This has been crucial in understanding my own positionality as a researcher, and especially as a middle-aged, white, male, English-speaking, heterosexual, able-bodied academic.

To achieve impact, the relationship skills you need to build strong and lasting networks are more important than any academic expertise you may have spent years honing. By remaining in touch with key people on a regular basis, you will be made aware of key policy developments and opportunities as they arise, enabling you to identify windows of opportunity that pass others by. However, it is worth pointing out that there are alternative approaches to the insider, relational approach I am suggesting in this chapter. There are a number of purposes and contexts that may warrant a more outsider approach, in which your role is to question and oppose policy, sometimes in antagonistic ways. However, I think we can think too simplistically about this as a binary choice, when in fact it is possible to switch between insider and outsider roles adaptively. This only works when you start as an insider, hence my emphasis on relational approaches in this chapter and throughout this book.

Amy Sanders, writing in her 2023 article in *Societies*, shows how third-sector organisation often combines insider and outsider strategies to great effect, with individuals maintaining close working relationships with key policy colleagues to influence change incrementally from the inside while working with their organisation on briefings that were harshly critical of the government. Fascinatingly, by using participant observation methods, Sanders found evidence of individuals switching between insider and outsider strategies within the same meeting, something I have witnessed in many such meetings myself. One of my mentors, Clifton Bain, who until recently was Policy Director of the charity I volunteer for, will work collaboratively with policy colleagues (in fact, I might even describe his tone as conspiratorial). And yet, in the same meeting, he will fundamentally question their assumptions and oppose certain ideas vigorously. And yet, he does this with such friendliness, and on the basis of such professional integrity and trust, that nobody holds anything against him, even if they still disagree with him just as strongly as he does with them. Rather than seeing this as hypocritical, it is possible to adopt this approach with integrity if you are transparent about the evidence and values that underpin your decision to switch between insider and outsider approaches.

CHAPTER **6**

Managing power dynamics

Ultimately, power in policy networks lies with those who make policy decisions. However, there is no single policymaker making all the decisions rather teams of people, often spread across different departments and agencies, working with ministers, politicians and policy advisors. Some of these people may have the power to frame the policy problem in relation to a prevailing narrative, reframe the issue, put policy options on the table or remove them and in various other ways influence the ultimate policy outcome. In this context, most researchers have very limited power to influence policy decisions.

However, as an expert in your field, you may have more access to policy officials and be more likely to be listened to than many of the people who will ultimately be affected by the policies you are engaging with. There is a tension at the heart of the concept of evidence-based policy-making between reliance on evidence from experts (which tends to focus on the effectiveness of policy outcomes) versus diversity of inputs from multiple people including those who will be affected by the policy (which focusses more on the inclusivity of the policy-making process). In this chapter, I want to ask how we might take an approach to policy that draws on our expertise as researchers, while managing the power dynamics that exclude certain voices from the policy process. As I argued in Chapter 3, it is this combination of top-down expertise and more bottom-up engagement with affected populations and the organisations that represent their interests that enable us to achieve more responsible policy impacts.

Justyna Bandola recently argued in her 2020 paper in *Evidence and Policy* that it is this combination of recognisable expertise and the usefulness of research in policy that gives researchers so much legitimacy in the policy arena. However, she points out that policy colleagues

DOI: 10.4324/9781003494942-7

she interviewed were unlikely to listen to researchers who focussed primarily on their technical expertise, who as a result often provided long, unintelligible reports or were too detached to be politically insightful. Correspondingly, those who prioritised the perspectives of affected populations over methodological rigour ran a similar risk. Effective co-production of research involving those who might ultimately be affected by a policy can help bridge the gap between expertise and usefulness. Where this is not possible, it may be possible to co-produce policy recommendations with these groups or collaborate with organisations that are already working with them to produce joint outputs that are both evidence-based and inclusive. The perceived independence of researchers (which I will question later) gives us convening power, and it may be possible to bring people together who have never interacted before, to help inform our approach to policy. In addition to learning from these interactions ourselves, we can facilitate learning between those we bring together and generate ideas that are more likely to be heard and actually work.

WHAT VALUES ARE YOU TAKING TO THE TABLE?

Many of the researchers I train prize their neutrality, independence, distance and objectivity as their main source of legitimacy when working with policy. This independence can be an important source of legitimacy in many policy settings where there are few independent voices. As Justyna Bandola's work shows, our expertise is certainly valued by our policy colleagues, but I regularly question researchers and policy colleagues alike who tell me that the process of informing or influencing policy is or should be entirely apolitical. To paraphrase Paul Cairney in his book, *The Politics of Policy Analysis* (2021), from which I have drawn heavily in this text, any attempt to characterise policy engagement as anything other than political is an exercise in power that attempts to downplay the politics of knowledge production and use.

I would argue that we are being political and exercising power whenever we choose to include or exclude informal, experiential knowledge and focus only on evidence from research. Which problems should be prioritised and on what basis? Perhaps a more telling question would be to ask, 'who's problems should be prioritised'. To help us unpack this, Carol Bacchi devised six questions to critically examine how problems are identified and framed in policy, in her 2009 book, *Analysing Policy: What's the Problem Represented to Be?*:

1. How is the problem represented in the policy?
2. What assumptions underlie this representation of the problem?
3. How did this representation come about?
4. What is left unproblematic in this problem representation? Where are the silences and could the problem be thought about differently?
5. What effects are produced by this representation of the problem?
6. How and where has this representation of the problem been produced, disseminated and defended? How could it be questioned or disrupted in these different contexts?

Taken together, these questions can help us reflect on the assumptions and values underpinning:

- The representation of a problem;
- How its representation limits what can be talked about; and
- Who is relevant and the kinds of power that are shaping the framing of the problem (which could potentially be challenged).

These questions challenge the idea that we can make objective, value-based assessments of the best solution to a policy problem. Cost-benefit analyses are regularly employed for this purpose but implicitly give economics greater weight than any other criteria. While it is possible to expand the diversity of criteria used to assess policy options, it is often less easy to operationalise them. For example, if equity is introduced as a criterion, who chooses, on what basis do they choose which groups should be included (e.g. needs based) and what evidence should they use (e.g. easily available but contested secondary data versus costly new primary data collection or self-assessment of need)?

The goal is for us to become more self-aware as researchers of our own values, beliefs and assumptions, and our privilege and power, and how these implicitly influence our choices and judgement. To find out how self-aware you are, ask yourself the following questions:

- Who is ultimately in charge of your research and whose interests does it serve? What is the balance between you as the researcher, your funders and the people who might ultimately benefit from the work?
- Who designed its questions and scope and how did you decide what to focus on or exclude?
- Who designed your methods and chose what data to collect, where and how? To what extent were these decisions determined by the kind of funding you received, the sort of journal you want to get published in and the academic contribution you want to make versus its usefulness in policy and practice?
- Who will interpret the findings, how will they decide themes to discuss and whose perspectives will they use to interpret the meaning and significance? To what extent will these be other researchers like you, researchers from outside your discipline or non-academic perspectives which could help determine the meaning and significance of your findings for policy or practice?
- To what extent do you attempt to generalise your findings and why? Are you trying to reach a more international research audience or are you trying to make your research relevant to national or international policy agendas? While this may be more likely to achieve both academic and policy impacts than context-specific work adapted to local contexts, it may inadvertently benefit majorities as the expense of minorities.
- Who will you disseminate your research to and how will you adapt your work to ensure it can be understood and used by people outside academia?

I am fortunate enough to have started my career in conservation because researchers in this discipline are very aware of the values underpinning their work. As a consequence, my environmental research typically answers questions posed by people seeking to protect or restore nature rather than those seeking to grow the economy. I will provide you with rigorous research on how to protect or restore a habitat, but you'll have to go to an economist if you want to find out how much it will cost or assess the impact it could have on jobs or the local economy. I am not trying to obscure the costs of conservation – they just aren't in scope for my research. I used to claim that much of my research was co-produced with local communities, but I am now more open about the fact that I led the project and called the shots, often to ensure we delivered what our funders were looking for. However, I am also open about the fact that I often integrate natural science insights with knowledge from the people living and working in the landscapes I study and sometimes get their help interpreting my findings using methods like multi-criteria evaluation. The purpose of all my projects is to deliver impact, so even if the people living in that landscape don't receive copies of the research, they will experience some other kind of benefit. I have helped integrate my research into a series of short briefing papers via the charity I work with, but the average farmer is more interested in the new income streams they can access to restore peatlands.

By becoming more aware of our own values and privileges, we can avoid inadvertently framing problems and selecting options that further marginalise and exacerbate inequalities. The more we do this, the more aware we are likely to become aware of the underlying drivers of other decisions, so we can make them explicit and question them. As such, a key role for researchers in policy development is clarifying the values implicit in the arguments we make and hear, and facilitating debate, to increase the quality of decision-making.

This can make for some awkward conversations. I was once approached by the English government to write a review that would draw a line under a particularly contentious debate. Proponents from both sides of the debate were vigorously lobbying government with opposing proposals, and they wanted an independent report they could cite as the basis for coming down clearly on one side of the debate. The person who approached me claimed that they thought I was the only person who had the academic credentials and was viewed as impartial by people on both sides of the debate (personally I could think of a number of others they might have already approached, so I suspected flattery). I started by explaining that although I looked impartial, a quick look at my CV would show that I had been programme director for a BSc Environmental Conservation and worked part-time as Research Lead for a conservation charity. I was clearly on the conservation side of this particular debate.

But ultimately, having first-hand how people from the other side of the debate had vicitmised their chief scientist when he took sides, and the impact this had had on his mental health, there was nothing they could do to persuade me to take the job. Although the 'Reed Review' would have had a nice ring to it, no impact is worth your mental health. Instead, I gently suggested that they were more honest about the fact that they had already decided which side of the debate they were going to side with and that this was why they had approached me. As soon as they took sides, the losing side would probably request a judicial review and tie them up in legal knots. The evidence might not be water-tight on either side of this debate, but ultimately they needed to make a political decision, and based on their values, their instincts were to prioritise public over private good, and that was a good enough basis for action while the research caught up.

DECOLONISING RESEARCH FOR POLICY IMPACT

For most researchers, the link between their research and their values isn't that obvious. And yet, Western values are pervasive in research if we care to look at the way we value written outputs over the oral traditions that have conveyed knowledge for generations in many other cultures. There are systemic issues that make it difficult to facilitate both respectful and effective collaborations between researchers in more and less research-intensive institutions around the world. There are now many examples of 'parachute' or 'helicopter' research, as it has been called, where teams from research-intensive institutions, often from high-income countries that grew rich through their previous colonial exploits, collect data in another country, often of lower income, and then complete the research in their home country without any further engagement with or any tangible benefits for researchers or society in that country. In an attempt to address this challenge, some researchers now share authorship with local researchers in recognition of logistical or other support that facilitated the data collection. However, without meaningful engagement in the research design (and even sometimes even data collection), and often without any (significant) input to the publication itself, it can be argued that this approach is tokenistic. Moreover, such approaches hide the real problem of research that is extractive, delivering benefits primarily to the lead author (who is typically from a research-intensive institution and/or high-income country) without building capacity for research of a similar calibre among local teams, who remain dependent on overseas researchers for publications in top journals, perpetuating (often colonial) dependencies.

Reasons for limited engagement of researchers from less research-intensive institutions, especially in lower income countries, are complex, including the following:

- High undergraduate teaching loads during semesters (and sometimes over the summer break, typically working with postgraduate students);
- The need to work second jobs (e.g. consultancy) to supplement low incomes (often over the summer break);
- Difficulty reaching field sites due to lack of transport or travel budgets;
- Limited cash flow may mean payments are needed upfront to buy equipment or travel, and delays in payments reaching some countries may stall work or ultimately result in non-payment;
- Challenges collecting and analysing data due to a lack of (reliable or state-of-the art) research equipment and/or research permit;
- Political, public health, electricity supply or security challenges may prevent access to key people or data collection equipment, facilities or sites, and visa requirements may make it difficult for collaborators from low-income countries to visit high-income countries;
- Limited lab access and availability of research assistants and lab technicians to help with data collection and analysis;
- Limited professional services capacity creates barriers to obtaining research funding and delays in putting contracts in place to conduct work; and
- Limited access to (or time to engage with) research literature leading to unfamiliarity with new theories or methods that could help situate research on the cutting edge of the discipline.

If we are not aware of the hidden power dynamics between researchers from different backgrounds, then how can we even start appreciating the discrepancies in power that exist between research and policy elites and the populations they purport to serve? Chapter 5 will help you more systematically consider the (sometimes competing) interests, values, knowledges, beliefs, norms and worldviews of the people who might ultimately benefit from the policies you inform. In this way, it may be possible to avoid over-representing those most easily accessible to you and to represent, legitimise and amplify the diversity of perspectives and realities that are voiced by people who may be socially (or in other ways) distant to you.

There are a number of ways in which power can influence how knowledge is created, shared and used to generate policy impacts, including overt and covert forms of 'power within', 'power with', 'power to' and 'power over', according to Jo Rowlands, writing in *Development in Practice* in 1995. Table 6.1 describes each of these forms of power in turn, providing examples of how each might play out in policy settings.

When thinking about how to manage power dynamics in policy settings, I also find Steven Lukes's 2004 book *Power: A Radical View*, particularly useful:

- First, he suggests that the ability to influence decisions is typically overt and is typically viewed in instrumental terms as the ability of an actor to mobilise resources or other power bases to change a decision in their own self-interest. Of course, the power to influence decisions could be wielded by coalitions and alliances of organisations for a wide range of purposes.
- Second, we must also consider power to prevent decisions being made. This can be either overt or covert, for example by preventing particular groups being represented or topics being raised or narrowly framing issues in ways that exclude certain groups and their interests.
- Third, there is the ability to shape perceptions and preferences which is a more covert, subtle and slowly developing form of power to change hearts and minds, shaping values and beliefs, which in turn might shape decisions and actions.

Managing overt power in the policy impact generation process typically requires strategies such as negotiation, adaptation and compromise. Consider working with a professional facilitator who is experienced in working with conflict, or connecting with social movements, where possible led from the bottom-up, so your research is in service to self-determined goals from the group rather than your research career. On the other hand, more covert power dynamics require a deeper

Table 6.1 Types of power defined with examples based on Rowlands (1995) typology.

Type of power	Definition	Example
Power within	Power within refers to an individual's internal sense of self-worth, agency and confidence. It includes a person's ability to recognise and value their own strengths, perspectives and preferences, as they grow more self-aware and build self-esteem. This empowers people to make choices and decisions that align with their interests and values.	You might work with community or representative groups to foster 'power within', empowering marginalised or vulnerable groups so that they have agency and voice in the development of new policies. For example, in education policy, this could include implementing programs that encourage student participation in decision-making, offering diverse and inclusive curriculum that reflects students' identities and experiences and providing resources for mental health support. By nurturing students' self-worth and confidence, education policy can empower them to become active participants in their own learning and personal development.
Power with	Power with refers to collaborative and collective power. It involves individuals forming alliances, networks and communities to achieve shared goals. This kind of power focuses on the strength that emerges when people work together, share their experiences and create connections. It recognises that collective action can amplify individual voices and create more impactful change.	You might form alliances or join existing networks of organisations who are working together and collectively have 'power with' the policy teams they work with. For example, this could involve creating spaces for collaboration between government agencies, environmental organisations, local communities and businesses. Instead of imposing top-down regulations, policies could be developed through participatory processes that involve these wider networks of organisations. This collaborative approach ensures that various perspectives are considered and that decisions are collectively shaped, leading to more effective environmental policies.
Power to	Power to refers to the capacity to take action and make decisions that influence the course of a persons' own life and the lives of others. This kind of power highlights the importance of having the means and resources necessary to exercise agency and achieve goals. It is about empowerment through access to education, resources, opportunities and the ability to participate in decision-making processes.	You might work to give 'power to' certain groups through new policies. For example, in employment policy, this might happen by promoting workers' rights, fair wages and access to training and skill development. Policies that support labour unions, advocate for workplace safety and ensure equal pay for equal work contribute to empowering workers with the ability to negotiate for their interests. Policies that aim to give power to workers may also focus on reducing barriers to entry into the job market, providing opportunities for upward mobility and addressing systemic inequalities that hinder individuals' access to meaningful employment.

(Continued)

Table 6.1 Types of power defined with examples based on Rowlands (1995) typology. *(Continued)*

Type of power	Definition	Example
Power over	Power over is the traditional and often negative dimension of power. It involves dominance, control and authority exerted by one group or individual over others. This form of power can lead to inequalities, exploitation and the suppression of voices and rights. Power over is about maintaining hierarchies and enforcing compliance with established norms.	You might work towards policies that grant public bodies and other organisations or groups with 'power over' others or certain types of decision. Those with the ability to oppose such policies may use power over strategies if they initiate a legal challenge to a new law, or work with opposition parties to overthrow the ruling party, as a way of changing a policy that compromises their interests. For example, criminal justice policy might attempt to reform dominant 'power over' dynamics in the system by moving towards restorative justice models. Instead of focusing solely on punishment and control, policies might prioritise rehabilitation, community reintegration and addressing the root causes of crime. By reducing the power of the state over individuals through mass incarceration, discriminatory practices and excessive use of force, these policies might further promote fairness, accountability and social reintegration.

understanding of the existing values, beliefs, histories and agendas of the people you are working with. As Paul Cairney writes in *The Politics of Policy Analysis*, '*the most profound and worrying kinds of power are the hardest to observe*' (2021, p. 88). These are especially hard to spot if your values align with those in power. To make the values and beliefs of those you are working with explicit, you might consider running a pre-workshop questionnaire to identify values and discuss these explicitly through storytelling exercises. To subtly manage power imbalances, you may try and reframe issues and positions to legitimise marginalised groups and their interests.

WHERE DOES CHANGE COME FROM?

By engaging with more diverse groups and perspectives, it may be possible to come up with new approaches to old policy problems. Some of my own early research suggested that this happens because you increase the diversity of information inputs to a decision. Research by Mieke Snijder and Marina Apgar published by the Institute for Development Studies in 2021 explain this as the process of synergy, where different perspectives, resources and skills are combined to derive new ideas. A 2023 study led by Jens Newig, published in *Global Environmental Change*, analysed the impact of participation on environmental outcomes in 305 case studies around the world. They found that the key predictor of positive outcomes was the extent to which power was delegated to participants. This echoes research I published with Joris de Vente and others in *Ecology & Society*, which identified the use of professional facilitation to manage power dynamics as a key success factor. Snijder and Apgar also emphasised the importance of creating safe spaces in which people from different backgrounds can share their perspectives. To do this well takes time, as it takes time for a group to build trust and empathy, navigate power differences sufficiently to engage in critical dialogue and be vulnerable enough to share and learn from each other. To do this sort of work, an experienced facilitator is needed with time dedicated to relationship and trust-building exercises.

Done badly, such well-meaning attempts at inclusivity can allow some voices to dominate or undermine others, exacerbating conflict and damaging relationships. Roger Few, in his 2001 *Geographical Journal* article, described a situation, which he termed 'containment of participation', where more powerful individuals or groups can consciously or subconsciously steer engagement processes towards support for a specific method or a predetermined outcome, by forging tactical alliances and blocking dissent. Done well however, more inclusive approaches to the generation of policy impacts can enable people to envision their own futures and seize their own power rather than waiting for top-down policy solutions to reach them. Our role is to facilitate the changes that are needed, and sometimes grassroots engagement like this shows us that we have been looking for change in the wrong places. If it is possible to facilitate change from the bottom-up, then policy change may not be necessary.

Indeed, it may not even be desirable if we no longer believe in the political system itself. Given the lack of a realistic choice for anything other than parties that support continuing economic growth, which we know is the main cause of climate breakdown and the destruction of nature, I share these doubts. As a result, I recently decided to declare my own politics, joining the Scottish Green Party and financially supporting youth activist group, New Green Deal Rising (I'm too old to join). Instead of helping those who are marginalised to engage with a broken political system, perhaps we should be empowering them to take action themselves? As Farhana Sultana put it in her 2023 article in *Geo: Geography and Environment*:

> The planetary crisis is a colonial capitalist product. Decolonising the current system is not about more diversity. It is not about having a seat at the table, but burning the table down and a fundamental reformulation of paradigms and solidarities rooted in justice....

In reality, I think we need both bottom-up and top-down approaches. I have worked with many governments around the world, but in recent years, I have focussed my efforts on helping policy colleagues in Scotland (where I live), England (where most of the people in the UK live) and working on peatlands with the United Nations Environment Programme (I'll share an embarrassing story about how that relationship started later in the book). At the same time, I have been trying to work from the bottom-up to help overlooked habitats, species and local communities that have no political voice. I am just a small part of a much larger team in the peatland charity that has succeeded over the last decade in pushing a previously forgotten habitat up the policy agenda, contributing to the protection of ground-nesting birds like Golden Plover and Curlew and birds of prey like Hen Harriers. In my local town, I am a volunteer board member for Huntly Development Trust, where we are generating our own funds via community renewable energy projects alongside government grants to regenerate our town centre and provide rural bus services that the government is no longer supporting to help people get into town for doctor appointments and shopping. I've recently also become a volunteer board member for Landscape Enterprise Networks, a company that aims to use funding from ecosystem markets to benefit farmers and their local communities on a much larger scale, while restoring landscapes and transitioning farming to more regenerative practices. In the charity, development trust and company, we are getting on with the job of helping those in need, and although we'll take help from governments where it is available, we will do the work from the bottom-up, with or without help.

I will confess that I struggle to find as much time as I would like to devote to these causes, but the more I have engaged at the grassroots, it has become more and more easy to justify investing this time as I have seen how this work feeds back into my research and policy work.

I am asking more critical research questions, with ready-made case studies for funding proposals that get me the peer-reviewed papers and funding I need to justify investing more time on impact to my university managers. And by representing the unheard voices of local communities and non-human species to my policy colleagues, I am able to identify challenges and opportunities they are blind to that I too would not have noticed had I not understood the realities on the ground to the extent that I now do.

My hope is that you too, by interrogating the values you bring to your research, will be able to become more self-aware and engage more consciously with the things you care about most deeply, in both your research and policy work. When you do so, your enthusiasm will become infectious, enabling you to justify investing more time doing what you love most with others who share your passion. You will be able to see power dynamics you were previously unaware of, and by managing these, you will be able to choose when to work with the ruling elites and when to step out of the circles of power and just get the job done.

Part 2
Strategic policy impact

CHAPTER 7

Is it appropriate to engage with policy yet?

In Part 1 of this book, I have proposed what I think is a more responsible approach to policy impact than we often see in practice. In addition to principles and approaches, I have shared tools and skills to help you work with complexity, navigate relationships and manage privilege and power. In the rest of the book, I want to remain practical, starting in this chapter by helping you choose your influencing strategy, mode of engagement and the kinds of role you feel most comfortable playing in your policy networks.

CHOOSING AN OVERALL STRATEGY

I have already emphasised the importance of looking beyond the kinds of evidence that typically arise from research, to take a more inclusive approach to impact that is able to deal with uncertainty and complexity. As researchers, however, our rigour of our research and the evidence it can produce are at the heart of the unique contribution we can make to policy. As a result, before getting too excited about policy impacts, it is important to assess whether you should be aiming to achieve impact yet or whether in fact such a strategy would be premature, and you should focus instead on the research necessary to build a stronger evidence base.

Therefore, when choosing the right overall strategy, you should first assess how strong the evidence is, both around the nature of the problem and the proposed solutions (Figure 7.1). No matter how conclusive, if your study is the only of its kind, I would question the strength of the evidence base. It is always possible that future studies may contradict your work for valid reasons, for example because they used equally credible but different theory or methods, had a different sample or studied a different

DOI: 10.4324/9781003494942-9

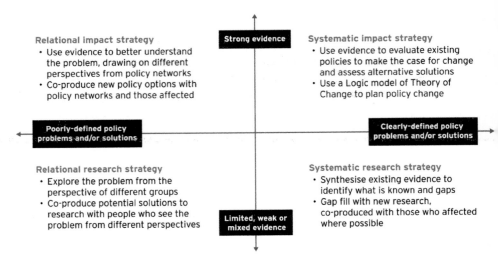

Figure 7.1 How to adapt your research or impact strategy to the strength of evidence and extent to which policy problems and solutions are well-defined.

part of the system at a different time or over a different timeframe. If there is limited, weak or mixed evidence and the policy problem and solutions are well-defined, then it may be possible to pursue a fairly **systematic research strategy**, synthesising existing evidence to identify what is known and the gaps, and then gap filling with new research, where possible co-produced with those who are affected by the problem. On the other hand, if the policy problem and solutions are poorly defined and the evidence is also poor, you may need to take a more **relational research strategy**, working with social scientists or colleagues from the arts and humanities to explore the problem from perspective of different groups in society, before co-producing potential solutions that could be researched in collaboration with people who see the problem from different perspectives.

Where there is strong evidence, it is possible to turn your attention to impact. If the policy problem is clearly defined and also well researched and understood, and there are a number of clearly defined policy options with a strong evidence base, then it is possible to develop a **systematic impact strategy**. In this case, you might use evidence to evaluate existing policies, to make the case for change and assess alternative solutions, before using a Logic Model or Theory of Change to plan policy change (more on these methods later). On the other hand, no matter how strong your evidence, if the policy problem and solutions are poorly defined, you will need to take a more **relational impact strategy**. In this case, you might use evidence to better understand the problem, drawing on different perspectives from across your policy networks, before co-producing new policy options with members of those networks and those affected by the issue.

TOOLS FOR IMPROVING THE EVIDENCE BASE

If you are unable to move to an impact strategy yet, based on Figure 7.1, due to a limited, weak or mixed evidence base, then you will need to adopt a research strategy. Evidence synthesis is a useful starting point because it can both assess the quality of existing evidence and, where there is sufficient evidence, provide robust new insights that could form the basis for policy development.

Evidence synthesis methods help you systematically integrate findings from multiple studies to generate reliable insights on a given topic. There are several types of evidence synthesis methods, which are relevant to different types of research questions and goals, for example:

1. A scoping review maps the available literature on a broad topic, providing an overview of the key concepts, types of evidence and research gaps. It can help you identify the extent and distribution of existing evidence and help you develop a more focused systematic review.
2. Systematic reviews involve a rigorous and structured approach to identifying, selecting, appraising and synthesising existing studies answering a specific research question. It aims to provide an unbiased and comprehensive overview of the available evidence.
3. Meta-analysis is a statistical method that is often used in systematic reviews to analyse data from multiple studies and provide a quantitative summary of the combined results, enhancing statistical power and enabling you to spot trends, patterns or differences that might not be apparent in individual studies.
4. Realist reviews focus on understanding the underlying mechanisms that explain the outcomes of complex interventions. They go beyond just assessing the effectiveness of interventions to try and explain how and why certain interventions work (or don't) in different contexts.

5. Qualitative evidence synthesis methods, such as thematic synthesis or meta-ethnography, systematically analyse and integrate qualitative research findings by identifying common themes from across a body of qualitative studies. They may be combined with more quantitative methods as part of a mixed-methods synthesis.
6. An umbrella review summarises systematic reviews and meta-analyses on a specific topic, providing a high-level perspective on the state of knowledge in a particular area.
7. Rapid reviews are truncated versions of systematic reviews that are often used to inform policy because they can be conducted relatively quickly. They attempt to maintain similar standards of rigor as a systematic review but are necessarily more narrowly focussed, with streamlined search strategies.

Rapid reviews were developed to reduce the time and cost of doing systematic reviews. A 2019 study by Matthew Michelson and Katja Reuter published in *Contemporary Clinical Trials Communications* calculated that a typical systematic review costs about £100,000 and takes between 6 months and 16 months assuming five co-authors devote 10-20 hours per week to the review. In contrast to this, I recently helped run a series of rapid reviews which cost an average of £2336 per review. Our programme also sought to provide early career researchers (ECRs) with the necessary skills to do rapid reviews.

Working with international evidence synthesis expert, Dr Gavin Stewart from Newcastle University, we created a synthesis training programme for ECRs with the University of Leeds and N8 AgriFood. Gav ran two workshops for a total of 30 researchers to train them in synthesis techniques. I elicited policy needs and evidence gaps from the policy community, which we turned (where possible) into questions that could be answered using evidence synthesis. Gav and I then supported each group to produce a peer-reviewed synthesis and policy brief. Each researcher left the process with new skills and a paper, the cost per synthesis and policy brief were tiny and because the policy briefs targeted questions that arose directly from the policy community, there is real potential for impact.

It is worth noting that while each of the above approaches is usually based on literature searches, they may each be informed by interviews with the authors of the literature they cite and perspectives from others with relevant expertise via interviews, focus groups or surveys, for example where there is a significant amount of 'grey literature', unpublished data or groups whose voices are important to the issue but not represented in the peer-reviewed literature. For example, I was recently asked to provide some policy advice on a topic I didn't fully understand, so I applied for £10K to pay a colleague to review the literature and organised an online roundtable with over 60 people from the investment, policy, landowner, third-sector and rural communities. They were given our literature review in advance and were invited to discuss and supplement the findings with their own perspectives at the event, leading to 16 policy options, a number of which are currently being pursued by Scottish Government. It may feel risky and vulnerable to provide advice when you do not have all the expertise you would ideally want. However, I would argue that you just have to have enough expertise to interrogate the literature and know who to ask for help, and with the collective knowledge of the literature and your networks behind you, it may be surprising what becomes possible.

There are a number of other methods for appraising and synthesising evidence that are worth mentioning. Many simply help you assess the quality of individual studies using standard criteria. For example, the Critical Appraisal Skills Programme host a number of checklists you can use to evaluate the quality of randomised controlled trials, economic evaluations and qualitative, cohort and case control studies. There are also frameworks that suggest rankings of methods, typically favouring randomised controlled trials as their gold standard. However, such frameworks tend to be heavily biased towards objectivist approaches, often downplaying the credibility of qualitative approaches and many methods from the arts and humanities, which for some purposes and contexts may in fact be the most relevant and reliable approach, providing rich descriptions and explanations of causal factors that may not be possible using any other method.

If you have tried to do an evidence synthesis, and it has become clear that there is insufficient evidence, you may need collect new primary data. Although much of the research you may need to do will require funding, it may be possible to integrate some of this work into an existing research project or do small tasks unfunded, as you have time. Your choice of research design and methods will need to reflect both your purpose and context. While the purpose will differ according to the issues you are researching, we all have the challenge of adapting to a context in which timeliness is valued as much as rigour. Some questions will inevitably take years to answer, but where there is a quicker, equally rigorous option, for example synthesising existing evidence, this should always be considered. Your choice of methods will dictate the time and resources needed, the number of assumptions necessary and ultimately both the rigour and timeliness of your outputs.

Figure 7.2 provides a taxonomy of methods that can help you explore how different groups define policy problems and relevant solutions. First you will need to choose the epistemological approach you are most comfortable with, noting how your choice may limit the kinds of questions you will be able to ask. Objectivist methods will help you describe, predict and objectively evaluate policy problems and potential solutions. More subjectivist methods will help you uncover perceptions and different ways of understanding the policy problem, how it is likely to evolve and the likely outcome of alternative solutions for different groups. Alternatively, you may want to choose a combination of both objectivist and subjectivist methods, and there are some mixed-methods approaches that are able to integrate data generated in very different ways. For example, in some of my projects I have used scenarios and complex systems models to integrate qualitative insights from semi-structured interviews with quantitative relationships derived from process-based models. Some of these methods are more useful for exploring how problems have evolved and how they are currently experienced. Other methods are more useful for understanding how problems are likely to evolve over time and the likely outcomes of alternative solutions to those problems. Some have the potential to provide insights into past, present and future dimensions of the problem and solutions.

Finally, I think it is important to reflect on the quality of our own research and whether it is really rigorous enough for us to make policy recommendations. We all believe that we are doing rigorous research, but issues with research rigour are among the most common things that can go wrong for researchers who want to influence policy. It is important to take particular care when communicating research that

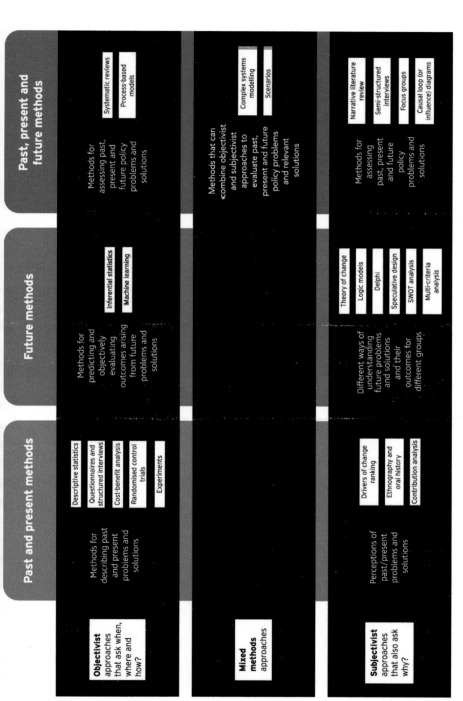

Figure 7.2 Taxonomy of methods that can explore how different groups define policy problems and relevant solutions.

has yet to go through the peer-review process. Although it is increasingly common to publish preprints of papers that are under review, if your findings are significant (especially if they are significantly different to previous research in the area) and you have any doubt about their rigour, it may be wiser to wait until you have your reviewers' feedback, even if that means you miss a window of policy opportunity. Is it really so urgent that you need to communicate this now, or could you wait? If your reviewers identify a major flaw in your work, it will not only be difficult to identify everyone who needs to know that your findings are no longer valid but also it will be professionally embarrassing.

The other major temptation for researchers who are under increasing pressure to publish in top-ranked international journals is to overclaim or over-generalise your conclusions. This might get you into a top journal in your field, but it might also get you into serious trouble if someone actually tries out your policy recommendation in the real world. Researchers are increasingly making policy recommendations in their research outputs, especially in more applied journals, but real care is needed here. Policy should not be based solely on the findings of individual studies. If it is, then policies will flip-flop as soon as another study is published with contradictory findings. This is why policies are ideally based on evidence synthesis. As a result, you should refrain from making speculative policy recommendations on the basis of your latest study. If you do wish to make suggestions, then if possible frame them as policy options (rather than recommendations), emphasising the limitations of the research and any uncertainty, and where possible put your findings in the context of the wider literature via a short narrative review or something more systematic.

CHAPTER **8**

Strategic approaches to policy impact

If there is already strong enough evidence, then it is possible to move to an impact strategy. Whether you plan to follow a systematic or a relational strategy, there are a number of tools you can use to help you plan for impact. Each of these tools builds on the 3i analysis from Chapter 5. Once you have identified and prioritised the people you think are most relevant to engage with, you will need to reach out to a handful of them (I usually start with three or four meetings), adapting your pitch to their interests to secure meetings.

When you are face-to-face or on a call with each other, you can step into their shoes much more effectively. Try and remain in listening mode as far as possible so that you can understand their context, including their hopes and fears, and their perspective on the issues you have been researching. Remain curious so that you can really understand where they are coming from. Now from this place of empathy, you can start identifying with them, the key problems they want to solve and the key benefits they want to see for their organisation or those they serve. It is important to listen out for different ways of framing the problem and different policy options that these groups might prefer based on that framing so that you can research and represent these different perspectives rather than attempting to find the 'right' way to frame the problem or the 'optimal' solution for any one group. In particular, consider if any of the groups you have identified might be systematically disadvantaged, for example on the basis of gender or race, and consider in your conversations with them how you might be able to analyse policy options from their perspective to avoid outcomes that further marginalise or oppress these groups.

DOI: 10.4324/9781003494942-10

TOOLS FOR SYSTEMATIC IMPACT STRATEGIES

There are a number of systematic approaches to engaging with policy for impact that are proven to deliver impact, many of which started life in international development, where there has long been a strong emphasis on delivering policy impacts. The challenges and aspirations you have heard in your initial meetings now become impact goals for your work together. At this point, it is important to bear in mind that you will not have the time, expertise or resources to address every challenge and aspiration you hear. It is therefore important to manage expectations and have some ideas about future funding calls or colleagues who they might be able to discuss ideas with, if you think they are outside the scope of what you can do with them.

There are two families of tool that can help you turn this into an actionable plan:

- **Theory of Change** is a flexible approach that can help you envisage in diagrammatic form each of the impacts you want to achieve, which are arranged in causal chains from your research to impact-generating activities through to early and late-stage impacts. You can find out more about this tool in Further Reading.
- **Logic Models** are tables that enable you to think through the connection between your research, impact-generating activities and the achievement of impacts. In the Logic Model linked from Further Reading, you will also be asked to identify activity and impact indicators to help you monitor progress towards impact and get things back on track if they aren't going according to plan. It also asks you to think about risks and assumptions and how you might mitigate the risks of your impacts going wrong or delivering unintended negative consequences. Finally, it asks you to think about the resources and time needed for your impact-generating activities to help you plan for impact.

Table 8.1 shows a Logic Model I developed for a large four-year project working with government and the dairy industry to enhance its environmental sustainability. In the table, I have extracted one out of three impact goals we developed in collaboration with industry partners.

The impact goal is being achieved as more and more dairy processors and manufacturing companies commit to net zero targets and incentivise the farmers supplying them to reduce emissions. It is debatable how much of this can be attributed to our project beyond the approaches taken by Nestle and First Milk who have drawn heavily on our research, but given their significant share of the milk market, we've certainly achieved some impact. Although we successfully completed most of our planned activities, one failed when a relationship with one of our partners went sour. Denoted by XXXX in the Logic Model to protect their identity, my relationship with their CEO went sour, just as we were trying to submit the bid and we had to re-allocate their budget to other activities. It is important to hold onto plans like these lightly. You are unable to foresee how contexts will change or, in our case, how partners will behave, and it is essential that you are able to drop activities that you can see are not actually needed or that are no longer possible, switching your resources to new opportunities as they arise.

The benefit of a well-designed Theory of Change is that you can explore multiple alternative pathways that could enable you to reach your goal, and you can show more clearly how each activity links together to achieve your impact. Figure 8.1 shows a simple Theory of Change I developed for a project with the United Nations (UN) Environment Programme to enhance the quality of evidence informing peatland policy around the world. The two impacts are linked together and yet to be achieved: to conserve, restore and better manage peatlands through more evidence-based national policies around the world. So far, we have achieved the outputs and integrated these with the first UN Global Peatland Assessment. Our next step is to commission a series of evidence syntheses, using the cost-effective method I described in Chapter 7. This will involve eliciting peatland policy questions from governments around the world via our UN networks, and each will have its own Theory of Change leading from the evidence synthesis paper and associated policy brief to the policy impacts being sought by the governments that have posed the questions. Only at that point will we be able to see how realistic our ultimate impacts are. I have chosen to share this example because it is in progress, and I already know that our Theory of Change will need to be adapted if it is to succeed. Again, my message is to hold your plans lightly and continually adapt to changing circumstances and opportunities as they arise.

Table 8.1 Logic Model for a large four-year project working with government and the dairy industry to enhance its environmental sustainability (status is colour coded using a green, amber and red system to indicate whether impacts are achieved, in progress or not achieved respectively).

Impact goals	Target groups	Aspects of the research relevant to them	Activities to engage this target group	Indicators of successful engagement (and means of measurement)
Develop scalable new pricing models for the dairy sector based on payments for ecosystem services (PES) that can inform the development of new natural capital policy that promotes nature-based solutions to climate change	Dairy industry including Nestle, First Milk, Arla Foods and Dairy Crest Dairy farmers, including National Farmers Union and farmer networks National government departments and agencies and local councils Ecosystem service beneficiaries including publics, Cumbrian utilities companies, Network Rail, supermarkets, Cumbrian food and drink manufacturers, insurers and local businesses Third-sector organisations including Rivers Trusts, Game & Wildlife Conservation Trust, Innovation in Agriculture, XXXX, Local Nature Partnerships and Catchment Pioneers	Research will: • Identify cost-effective farm and food system-level interventions • Develop a scientifically robust evidence base on their impacts, synergies and trade-offs for biodiversity, vegetation, soil, water, animal health and milk production This is of interest to the dairy sector that wants to see measurable improvements in milk supply and sustainability and is interested in investing in natural capital to increase resilience to flood threats and climate change and demonstrate corporate responsibility Policy bodies are interested in how this could: • Increase resilience in response to Brexit • Meet policy objectives of 2011 Natural Environment White Paper, PES Action Plan and PES aspirations in Defra's 25-year plan Third-sector organisations are interested in opportunities to leverage additional funding to meet their wider objectives	Promote milk premium and related schemes to new entrants in areas supplying Nestle manufacturing plants Seminars in Westminster (with Natural England) and Edinburgh, supported by a policy brief in collaboration with other relevant projects from our funding programme Develop a proof-of-concept initial ecosystem service market trade with partners in the Eden catchment (around the Petteril and Ullswater) Promote the approach to other companies in the food and drink sector	Revisions to Farmed Environment Plan as part of Nestle's milk premium scheme promoted via Game and Wildlife Conservation Trust (scheme options available online) Attendance by identified priority teams and follow-up opportunities taken up by relevant teams (event records) Practical involvement from demand-side businesses; engagement with supply side (workshop attendance; model trading system) Business briefings produced to high standard (feedback on drafts from business community)

Indicators of progress towards impact (means of measurement)	Risks to activities (and mitigation)	Risks to impact (and mitigation)	Who is responsible and what resources are needed?	Status
Significant numbers of new scheme entrants (Nestle scheme records)	No new materials developed (3Keel to lead development)	No new scheme entrants (Nestle and First Milk to lead)	Nestle, First Milk, and GWCT	Completed successfully
Integration of findings to post-Brexit agriculture policy (citations and testimonials)	Poor attendance (work with Natural England to target Defra teams, advisory board members for Scottish Government)	Brexit does not happen or it does happen and there is no policy influence (work with N8 AgriFood and our funder's high level networks)	Mark with N8 Universities and funding programme secretariat	Completed successfully
Major private investment from at least one new company or a number of smaller investments (financial records)	Businesses don't see sufficient value in engaging (3Keel managing through building momentum via regional business leaders)	No new investment (work with Government and Nestle to create conditions necessary)	3Keel, Nestle and United Utilities	Completed successfully
Business survey before/ after briefings showing change in awareness and new practices (survey findings)	Business briefings are not produced (work with XXXX who have strong track record of producing such briefings)	Limited awareness or change in business practice (revise and re-launch materials and training based on feedback)	XXXX	Not delivered

(Continued)

Table 8.1 Logic Model for a large four-year project working with government and the dairy industry to enhance its environmental sustainability (status is colour coded using a green, amber and red system to indicate whether impacts are achieved, in progress or not achieved respectively). *(Continued)*

Impact goals	Target groups	Aspects of the research relevant to them	Activities to engage this target group	Indicators of successful engagement (and means of measurement)
			Input to relevant expert groups, consultations, select committees and boards, for example Defra's Social Science Expert Group and Scottish Government's Strategic Research Programme Board	Written and/or oral evidence provided as opportunities arise (citations in relevant documents)
			Engage with the Parliamentary Office of Science and Technology on POSTnote or write our own policy brief on 'Post-Brexit Resilience and Sustainability of UK Dairy Sector'	Production of POSTnote or policy brief (new materials online including project findings)

MANAGING RISK IN POLICY ENGAGEMENT

Systematic tools like Logic Models and Theory of Change can help you think through the likely consequences of your work, so are useful ways of identifying potential pitfalls on your planned pathway to impact. The Logic Model that I use (Figure 8.1) prompts me to think about risks systematically, so I can identify risks associated with each impact (e.g. negative unintended consequences for specific groups or in particular

Indicators of progress towards impact (means of measurement)	Risks to activities (and mitigation)	Risks to impact (and mitigation)	Who is responsible and what resources are needed?	Status
Integration of findings to post-Brexit agriculture policy (citations and testimonials)	Few relevant opportunities or insufficient time to engage with them (training and support for Post Doctoral Research Assistants to lead drafting of responses)	Brexit does not happen or it does happen and there is no policy influence (work with N8 AgriFood and GFS high-level network)	Mark with relevant Co-Investigators	Completed successfully
Integration of findings to post-Brexit agriculture policy (citations and testimonials)	Lack of interest from Parliamentary Office for Science and Technology (launch Global Food Security-branded policy brief at seminars in London and Edinburgh)	Brexit does not happen or it does happen and there is no policy influence (work with N8 AgriFood and GFS high-level network)	Mark with relevant Co-Investigators	Completed successfully

contexts) and impact generation activity (e.g., exacerbating conflicts and wasting people's time):

- Assess the risks of unintended consequences arising from policy options based on your research, based on your understanding of the evidence and where possible consultation with those identified in your 2i analysis who might be affected by the impacts you are seeking.

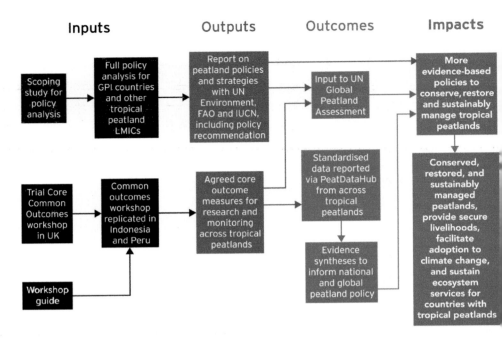

Figure 8.1 Theory of change for a project designed to conserve, restore and better manage peatlands through more evidence-based national policies around the world.

- Also assess the risks of each engagement activity you have planned. Again, feedback from the sorts of people you hope to engage can be invaluable. If this is not possible, get feedback from researchers or others in your networks who have more engagement experience than you.
- Continuously monitor and evaluate both your engagement and impact that can provide you with valuable early feedback when things are going wrong, which is why this is integrated into the impact planning template in the previous section: Tools for systematic impact strategies. By learning from mistakes, you can minimise your exposure to future risks. You will learn more about this in Chapter 13.
- Although it is good to have an impact plan, it is also important to be flexible and adapt your plans as circumstances change, responding to unforeseen challenges and opportunities.
- Although you only have to put your research through your institution's ethics committee if you are doing research with human subjects (not engaging for impact purposes), you may wish to take advice from ethics experts when you are working on particularly controversial issues or with vulnerable groups.

Before you ever get to an ethics committee though, I would encourage you to think deeply about your own personal values and ethics. What are you prepared to do, and where will you draw the line? It can help to explore this through discussion with others who are considering engaging more with policy or with those who already have policy experience in your field.

To ensure that you don't cross your own ethical red lines, when you are engaging with policy colleagues, it is important to learn how to instinctively work out when you might be approaching the danger zone. To do this, you need to cultivate a way to stay in the moment and reflect on your approach in real time when you are engaging with policy networks. In this way, you will be able to hold onto these values and ethics and immediately become aware when you are approaching an ethical red line before you inadvertently cross it. If you're not sure what you are looking for, think of a time when you made an error of judgement in your professional or personal life and think carefully about the moment before you made the decision that you lived to regret. Very often, there was a sense of unease that you couldn't quite put your finger on, and because you couldn't understand in your conscious mind why you shouldn't say 'yes' or do whatever it was that you did, you over-rode that feeling. However, in retrospect, had you paused long enough to examine that sense of unease, you may have become aware of the reasons for that subconscious warning and you might have acted differently. If nothing else, you might have found a way to play for time or postponed your decision until you could think about it a bit more. I feel it as a tightness in my chest, right before I act, or as queasiness or butterflies in my stomach in the lead up to that point. The next time you get that feeling, practise stopping to consider the source of your unease. The more you practise, the stronger this 'mindfulness muscle' will become, and this small step outside of yourself and the situation you are in will become second nature.

The reason it is so important to build a mindfulness muscle like this is that ethical red lines have a habit of creeping up on you unawares. Political traps tend to appear at the most unexpected times. Given that I am a member of the Scottish Greens, one of the most unexpected political traps I almost fell into was set for me by the former leader of the Green Party in England. I had just presented at a side event in one of the UN climate summits, and she asked the first question, specifically addressing me. As she spoke, I started to feel a rising sense of anxiety and shortness of breath, as my chest tightened, and I sensed that there was something wrong. This was the clue that something was wrong; my mindfulness muscle was tightening. Her question seemed straightforward on the surface, and it would have been easy to just attempt an answer. But I still sensed a political trap opening up somewhere in her question that I couldn't quite pinpoint, so instead of answering the question, I told her I was formulating my answer, and as I did so, I wondered if any of the other members of the panel, sitting at the front with me, wanted to share their views. One of the other speakers was happy to oblige and promptly fell into her trap. As soon as he started speaking, I could see the trap that had alluded me until then, that he was about to fall into. By the time he had finished speaking, I had formulated my own answer to the question that protected my integrity as a researcher and more importantly the credibility of the conservation charity and UN agency whose work I was presenting that day. By being aware of my body, I had been able to tap into my subconscious mind, which was telling me something was wrong. There was probably something I could have picked up on consciously in her tone of voice or micro-expressions, but in heat of the moment, our conscious minds often miss these clues, which are only picked up subconsciously.

Engaging with policy is never without risk, and as you grow in confidence and move from informing to influencing policy, the risks will increase along with the likelihood of impact. But so will the rewards, as you see your work contributing towards policies that deliver benefits across organisations and populations. A bit of fear is probably a good thing; the privilege of being able to shape policy should not be taken for granted, nor should it be used purely for the benefit of your policy colleagues or your own career. That's why in this book I propose an approach to policy impact that is responsible as well as strategic and practical.

By being mindful, you are doing the deep work of managing risk in your engagement with policy.

HOW TO PURSUE A RELATIONAL IMPACT STRATEGY

Relational strategies also build on your 3i analysis and the initial calls you have made. However, instead of trying to identify impact goals and strategies for reaching goals at the outset, this approach focuses more on building relationships and impact adaptively by helping people with issues and tasks, building trust and responding to opportunities for more significant impacts as these arise. In his PhD research, Noam Obermeister, Science-Policy Expert at Social Simulations, distinguishes between two types of relational strategy. He describes the first as 'networked intelligence' or the 'address book approach to science advice'. This kind of strategy is typically informal, loosely planned and adaptive and focused on building relevant networks and relationships of trust with key policy colleagues. For example, I have been asked if I could explain concepts and update new civil servants on the latest research in their area, help brainstorm questions for a consultation, find examples of things going wrong that could be used to make a case for regulation and comment on briefings to climate negotiators. Sometimes I am able to answer a question easily, and other times I will be able to find a review paper. If I'm not sure of the robustness of the evidence, say if I can only find one study or findings seem to be mixed across studies, I will caveat my advice and, if I have time, offer to do a short narrative review. This is only a day's work for most topics using the method I described in *The Productive Researcher*, and I can usually use it in the introduction of a paper at some point in the future. Moreover, I'm consolidating my own learning and growing in confidence in my role as a policy advisor. I once offered a morning of training to a policy team in return for an afternoon learning how to do a policy review from them (a handy skill for evaluating impact). I know of others who have given policy teams access to data or created decision trees or user interfaces to help them answer their own questions. This is useful when it is done in response to a question or need, but more often than not, these models are ignored and for good reason if you can't see the evidence and assumptions being used to generate the outputs.

The networked intelligence approach is typically a quite exclusive model, however, focusing on building networks and trusting relationships with members of the policy community, where possible those with decision-making power. However, Obermeister also identifies a 'collective intelligence' model in which 'the whole is greater than the sum of its parts', which focusses more on the diversity of perspectives you engage with, the range of voices you represent and the quality of deliberation you are able to facilitate between your policy colleagues and those in your wider networks. For example, you might discuss your research findings with community organisations or national NGOs and integrate your research with their perspectives as you learn from each other, either bringing policy colleagues into these debates or just sharing the insights that emerge. Following this approach with multiple organisations both within and beyond policy is time-consuming. However, it typically enables you to make more useful contributions to each organisation. Also, the work you do for different organisations has a habit of coalescing at various points in the process, enabling you to facilitate collaborations across your networks that can achieve impacts that would not have been possible by any organisation working in isolation. As such, the process is inductive where more systematic strategies are deductive, with impacts emergent rather than planned, consistent with what you might expect in any complex system.

If you have chosen organisations using a 3i analysis, there is a good chance that most of the people in these organisations will be connected to each other in some way, and sometimes senior colleagues in national NGOs have high-level access to political decision-makers, such as ministers. For example, Duncan Green from Oxfam writes in his book, *How Change Happens*, about one of his early policy impacts arose from an invitation to a dozen or so NGOs by the Chancellor of the Exchequer (in other countries, the Finance Minister or Treasury Secretary) to brief him directly on his negotiating position for the next round of world trade talks. I was once invited by an Environment Minister to talk and then debate head-to-head with the President of the National Farmers Union, representing the charity I volunteer for, to an invited audience of a hundred people, to inform the minister's approach to Brexit ahead of a speech she had to give at her party conference. Opportunities like this are rare for academics (other than this, the only interaction I've had with ministers is as they shake my hand and move on or via social media). But by working for organisations like these, you may get opportunities to brief those who have high-level access. Trust is crucial, however, as you are unlikely to be present when they communicate these findings, so you need to be sure that they won't cherry-pick, distort or in other ways manipulate your work for their own ends.

The key thing is that you deliver on the requests and opportunities that arise, to the timescale you agree with them and in a form that they can quickly and easily understand and use. If you don't have the expertise to provide what they've asked for, your responsibility is to find someone who has the relevant expertise (e.g. talk to your school impact officer) and ensure that they deliver something to time in a form that can be used. If you deliver, you produce a 'quick win' shared between you and your new colleague; you can build on this initial positive experience to generate longer term trust.

Between tasks, you can stay in touch, checking if there are other things you or your teams can help with, cementing your position in their mind as someone who they remember and call when they next need help. When they move to a new job, you will be in touch regularly enough to know that they are moving, so you can ask them to introduce you to their successor, who is instantly more likely to trust you by proxy. You might then offer them a call to brief them on the latest research in this area, to help ease them into their new job, while finding out how you can help them. This takes both time and commitment. If someone from your policy network contacts you for help and you don't respond, they might give you a second chance, but if you fail to respond the second time, it is unlikely you'll hear from them again. This means it is important to choose carefully and work hard to retain a small number of key relationships like this, so you have the time to prioritise their needs when they get in touch.

It is important that you do this for the public good and to help them rather than for your own career progression, funding or university. As I suggested in Chapter 1, the impact agenda has undermined trust in researchers. Unless we disclose the benefits of generating impact from our work with policy colleagues, this may lead to a later breach of trust when they discover that you or your institution will benefit from the work you are doing together. If it works, this approach enables you to build trust over time, and you are often recommended internally to other colleagues within the organisation, giving you increasing visibility across the teams you are working with and ultimately giving you opportunities to serve more senior decision-makers.

I have found that to be most effective, it is useful to take this relational approach with both civil servants and colleagues from organisations in the policy networks that are working on the same issues, starting with low-ranking colleagues and working your way to more senior colleagues slowly as you gain trust. In addition to national organisations working in the space, I also advocate for working directly with those affected by the issues you are working on. This doesn't need to be research work; it just needs to be real relationships with people who learn to trust you because you are genuinely there to try and help. In my case, this is typically farmers and community groups where I live in Scotland. Although I know that their experiences are unlikely to be representative of the rest of the country, the insights I gain and stories I am able to tell bring credibility and life to my research findings. I am no longer seen as out of touch, and in all honesty before speaking to people like these, I was out of touch with reality. Living in my academic bubble, it is easy to forget that there are many people, especially among the farming community, who do not believe that climate change is real and see the net zero agenda instead as a threat to their livelihoods and our food security as a nation. Working with people like this has enabled me to develop arguments that get sceptics on side without forcing them to change what they believe. In fact, a colleague from one of my policy networks recently told me that the most useful thing they learned from a briefing I gave to a National Farmer's Union Scotland was my approach to the sceptics rather than the evidence I was presenting.

Things don't always go my way, and I tend to learn even more from these bruising experiences. A company approached our local community, offering to rewild some of our land in return for an income from biodiversity and soil carbon credits, and given my expertise in this area, I offered to provide an assessment of the opportunity. However, knowing my positive views on carbon markets, one of my fellow board members invited Eleanor Harris, the Head of Natural Capital from Galbraiths, a company that regularly advises farmers on these issues. The fact that I was so surprised to lose the debate shows the pride and complacency with which I had approached the debate. I had expected to discuss the science, policy and markets, but Eleanor focussed on all the potential financial risks to the trust, while other board members focussed on the moral error of supporting offsetting when the climate crisis called for an actual change in our economy and how we live our lives.

This story is a useful example to illustrate a relational strategy to working with policy because I had built relationships across this particular policy network in a collaborative attempt to affect policy change. There was no clear Theory of Change at the start, other than the vague notion that we could extend what we'd learned about peatland carbon markets to other habitats and land uses to get funding for nature-based solutions to climate change on a much more significant scale than we were currently seeing. At the time, I was part of a network of universities in the north of England known as the N8 who had clubbed together to capture more funding and achieve more impact. A consultancy firm working with Nestle approached the university network with an idea for a research project, and I was asked to lead the £1.5M bid to the Global Food Security Programme, funded by UK Research and Innovation. We were successful, and during the project, Nestle suggested we use our research to create an agricultural soil carbon code that might work similarly to the Peatland Code. However, when we looked at the science, we concluded that there was insufficient evidence that the kinds of interventions being proposed were consistently helping the climate. We agreed to do a series of systematic reviews, but we were not ready to pursue impact. As such, we were pursuing a systematic research strategy, based on the fact that there was a well-defined policy opportunity but the evidence was mixed (the bottom right quadrant in Figure 7.1).

Before we had completed the evidence synthesis, however, we became aware of a number of companies already getting farmers to sell soil carbon, and we started getting approached by the more responsible companies in this space, who were looking for advice. This was a massively steep learning curve for me, as I began to realise that farmers were at risk from companies that might demand their money back when it transpired that there had been no appreciable change in soil carbon levels. More importantly, money that could be tackling climate change could be going into schemes that made no difference to the climate. The policy goal was gradually coming into focus; the government would need to create its own high-integrity soil carbon code that only allowed evidence-based interventions. We applied for government funding, as a group of academics, businesses and farmers organisations, to develop our idea. However, as soon as we started talking to policy colleagues and the companies already operating in the space, it became clear that a Conservative government was not going to create a publicly funded scheme that would put existing private schemes out of business (that would be anti-competitive). But our policy colleagues had a better idea, and we switched our project to focus on it instead. Rather than stifling competition in the market, our policy colleagues advised, we should be trying to regulate the market, forcing low-integrity companies to raise their game or cease trading. However, there were no existing regulations that could be used, and the complexity of the issue would make it difficult to create anything fit for purpose. It is easy to prove that you've grown a forest, but it is harder to prove that a restored peat bog or saltmarsh has stopped emitting greenhouse gases. You will need very different methods for regulating claims made about sea kelp compared to agricultural soil carbon. But again, our policy colleagues had an idea, and again we switched our project to explore this new idea. Ultimately, we produced recommendations for a new standard by which the quality of soil carbon schemes could be assessed, to be run by the British Standards Institute (BSI). Based on this proof of concept, BSI was then commissioned to create standards for carbon across multiple habitats and land uses, alongside standards for biodiversity and water quality markets, and I am now working directly with BSI to support that work. My ongoing work with farmers and my local community helped me devise the arguments I used to convince farmers from the National Farmers Union Scotland to take carbon markets serious whether or not they believed in climate change. This in turn led me to create a Frequently Asked Questions document for policy officials who were struggling to answer similar questions and being asked to brief ministers who had to be able to debate the issues more publicly. Most of this work happened after our £1.5M project had ended, and was done on a shoestring, but it has given me research questions and case studies for a series of large research proposals I'm currently developing. And so, the cycle will continue, following our noses, solving challenges as they arise, to feel our way towards the policy impacts that are actually needed, that nobody could have identified in a Theory of Change or Logic Model at the outset. Having said that, we did identify a number of impacts in the proposal for our big project, and once we got funding, I turned this into the Logic Model in Table 8.1. We actually did deliver on the majority of our planned impact goals. It's just that there was another much bigger impact that we couldn't see at the time.

The point I want to make is that neither approach is superior, and in reality, it is good to take both a relational and a strategic approach in parallel. You can't plan for everything and you can't leave everything to emerge inductively through your engagement with the policy system. The key issue when choosing your strategic approach is that it is tailored to the needs, interests and contexts of those you seek to help and that you engage with these groups over the long term. By co-producing an impact plan with members of relevant policy networks, you will be able to take a more strategic and empathic approach to your policy work. By building networks of people you can trust, you will be able to identify and adapt to new opportunities, remaining relevant and useful in an ever-changing policy context. Instead of dreaming up impacts in your ivory tower and wasting time on multiple pathways to policy impact that fail to deliver any benefits, you are able to prioritise the most important evidence gaps and policy needs, with the limited time you have for policy engagement. Instead of doing this by yourself, by building relationships with others in your policy network you are able to join forces and achieve levels of engagement and policy impacts that would have been impossible to achieve by yourself. By continuing your engagement with these groups over the long term, you are able to learn the 'rules of the game' in different policy organisations and processes, forming trusted networks on the basis of a track record of useful and reliable advice.

It is worth sounding a word of caution in conclusion, however. A researcher interviewed by Justyna Bandola for her 2023 paper in *Minerva* described the relational strategy like this:

> You do have to bend a lot more, in terms of your research design and what you want to do to the needs they have, some of which might just be practical …. You have less control as a researcher and its more intimate and more potentially political.

As a result, researchers interviewed by Bandola cautioned that research done in service to policy colleagues may be difficult to publish, given the differences in standards of rigour between research and policy worlds. I try and deliver outputs for policy colleagues to the highest possible standard so that they can subsequently be used in research outputs, but it doesn't always work out. It is worth being realistic about the fact that much of the work you do with and for policy colleagues may count for little in the academic system, as it currently stands.

CHAPTER 9

How to engage

Whether you have chosen to take a primarily strategic or relational strategy to your policy work, or a combination of the two, you also need to consider the mode of engagement and the kinds of role you feel most comfortable playing as you engage with your policy networks. In this chapter, I will help you to think about the extent you want to limit yourself to informing policy, or try and actually influence policy. I also want you to think deeply about the potential roles you could play as you inform and influence policy. This thinking will enable you to prioritise the activities you engage in and minimise the risks you will need to take. Researchers are regularly told that they need to get out of their comfort zone if they want to achieve impact, but I am going to suggest that you should only move as fast and far as you feel comfortable, as the personal and career risks of getting things wrong are considerable.

CHOOSING A MODE OF ENGAGEMENT

Broadly speaking, there are two modes of engagement that you can choose from when engaging with policy. Informing may be less likely to achieve impact, but it is less time-consuming and less risky, whereas influencing may take more time and be more risky, but it is more likely to lead to impact. Rather than looking for the right mode of engagement, your task is to work out what is the best fit for your career stage, type of research and personality. Looking at the horizontal axis in Figure 9.1, you first need to decide on your preferred mode of knowledge use, that is how you like to use your knowledge when working with policy colleagues:

- Do you prefer to provide evidence as a one-way transfer, or do you prefer to engage in two-way conversation, asking and answering

DOI: 10.4324/9781003494942-11

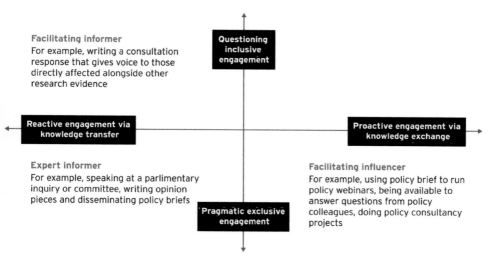

Figure 9.1 How to choose an appropriate mode of engagement with policy, depending on your preferred use of knowledge and level of inclusivity.

questions as you exchange knowledge with policy colleagues? For example, if you are an early career researcher (ECR), you may prefer the relative safety of knowledge transfer, given that you have deep enough expertise to provide advice but limited breadth of knowledge or experience to answer questions and engage in debate. Alternatively, despite the additional time and risk of engaging in two-way communication, do you want to get to know your policy colleagues, enjoy the intellectual stimulation or prefer to share knowledge in ways that enable you to adapt what you say to the needs of your audience?

· You also need to consider whether you prefer reacting to requests from policy colleagues, for example when there are consultations or calls for evidence, or if you also want to reach out more proactively to policy colleagues when you have evidence or ideas that are relevant to ongoing policy processes. You may prefer to have deadlines that give you time to plan your response to clearly formulated questions in more reactive mode. Alternatively, despite the additional time required to stay up-to-date with ongoing policy processes, do you prefer to be more involved in the policy teams you work with, offering evidence, ideas and help more proactively?

Next, you need to decide on your preferred mode of engagement:

- Do you prefer taking a pragmatic approach to engaging with policy colleagues, recognising the many constraints they are under and working with their framing of the policy problem and only those solutions that are politically feasible? Alternatively, do you naturally prefer to question the premise upon which the consultation has been written or the way your policy colleague has framed the problem or constrained the feasible solutions?
- Do you prefer working alone or with other experts, typically other researchers, in developing your advice to policy colleagues? Alternatively, despite the additional time involved, do you enjoy working with people and organisations outside academia and believe it is important to seek out and give voice to groups who might be affected by the issues you are working on, who might otherwise not be heard?

If you prefer working more reactively, transferring your knowledge in ways that don't require you to engage in open debate, then you will more naturally gravitate towards an **informing** mode of policy engagement. If you prefer to do this in a pragmatic way, based primarily on your own expertise and the expertise of other researchers, you are likely to find it comfortable being an **expert informer**. For example, you might speak at a parliamentary inquiry or committee, write opinion pieces or disseminate policy briefs. If you prefer to do this in a more questioning way, facilitating inputs from others in your wider policy networks and groups who might be affected by the issues you are working on, then you are more likely to be comfortable as a **facilitating informer**. For example, you might write a consultation response that gives voice to those directly affected alongside other research evidence.

On the other hand, if you prefer a more proactive approach to exchanging knowledge with your policy colleagues, then you will more naturally gravitate towards an **influencing** mode of policy engagement. If you prefer to do this in a pragmatic way, based primarily on your own expertise and the expertise of other researchers, you are likely to find it comfortable being an **expert influencer**. For example, you might use policy briefs to run policy webinars, make yourself available to answer questions from policy colleagues or apply to do policy consultancy projects. If you prefer to d this in a more questioning way, facilitating inputs from others in your wider policy networks and groups who might be affected by the issues you are working on, then you are more likely to be comfortable as a **facilitating influencer.** For example, you might create alliances with non-academic organisations, co-produce policy options with those affected by the problem or do consultancy projects for NGOs seeking to influence policy.

The safest place to start is informing policy, which I define as engaging reactively with policy through knowledge transfer. This is not without risk, as without engaging with anyone, it is possible for your published work to be used or misused by those seeking to shape policy. If your work is controversial and starts to be used by others in ways that you feel uncomfortable with, it may be a bigger risk to your reputation to do nothing than it is to start engaging actively with policy networks, to try and take back control of the narrative around your research. However, it is undoubtably less time and effort than taking a more proactive, two-way approach to engagement, which will require regular communication with policy teams who may ask difficult questions in response to the evidence you provide.

If you want to inform policy, the best place to start is the formal mechanisms established by the parliament or policy body you want to work with. There are many other books, websites and toolkits that you can consult for the country in which you are working, and as researchers work internationally, it would not be practical to include these in a book like this. While this information is easy to find in most countries and for international policy bodies like the Intergovernmental Panel on Climate Change, some countries are less transparent about how they work with researchers and evidence. In these cases, you will need to be guided by your in-country partners and your own ethics, depending on the advice you are given. In some cases, you may need to work via local researchers or other intermediaries, for example national charities and think tanks. I will cover a variety of these mechanisms in Part 3 of the book, but they include subscribing to relevant email lists so you don't miss deadlines for relevant policy consultations or inquiries. A consultation response may in turn lead to an invitation to give oral testimony to a legislative body, committee or inquiry. There are usually a range of committees and cross-party groups with chairs or secretariats you can engage with, and there are often opportunities to apply for roles as members of expert advisory committees, linked to your field of expertise.

However, it is hard to know if your consultation or inquiry response actually reached any relevant policy teams or if the inquiry or committee report that used your evidence was actually useful to these teams. Many consultations receive tens of thousands of responses, and when this happens, the policy teams will not read every response. Instead, someone in the team or an external consultant will provide them with a summary of the responses, pulling out key responses for them to read in full. There is a strong possibility that your carefully crafted response might be represented by a few words in the summary (or even worse, just appear in a word cloud).

This presents you with a moral dilemma. If your research is policy relevant and publicly funded, then you surely have an obligation to do your best to ensure relevant policy teams know about your work. If all you do is submit evidence to formal processes when requested by government, do you actually know that your evidence has reached the relevant teams? If not, is there a chance that research that could have been pivotal in making a policy decision gets inadvertently missed by the people who most needed to know about it?

It is for this reason that many researchers move from informing to influencing policy, which I define as proactive engagement with policy via knowledge exchange. There are overlaps between the methods and approaches you will use to inform and influence policy, and you should avoid bypassing the mechanisms designed by the parliaments and the organisations you are trying to influence. However, once you have used these mechanisms, if you think your evidence is particularly important, then the next step may be to ensure that key decision-makers really do have access to your work and understand its policy implications. The key differences between informing and influencing are shown in Table 9.1.

CHOOSING A ROLE

As you chose the role or roles you want to take in the policy networks you engage with, it is important to understand what your comfort zone is and why you feel uncomfortable with certain types of engagement. If you move rapidly beyond your comfort zone, you may take unnecessary risks and inadvertently cross ethical red lines that could be costly in terms of your reputation. However, if you are unable to be as effective as you want from your current comfort zone, it is possible to consider the skills

Table 9.1 Differences between informing and influencing modes of engagement.

Informing	Influencing
Takes limited time to send published research outputs to policy colleagues or turn these into a response to a request for evidence.	Takes time to translate published research into plain English relevant to a policy area, co-produce policy products (e.g. policy briefs and infographics) and build relationships with policy teams.
It is often difficult to know which questions in a consultation are most important or what language to use to ensure your evidence is understood.	As you build relationships across policy networks, you can get feedback on your policy communication to ensure you address the most important questions in language that will instantly resonate with policy colleagues.
There is limited risk to your reputation in one-way communication of research findings, though risks increase when you are invited to give oral evidence.	The more two-way and deep your engagement, the more likely you are to be asked questions that are beyond your expertise or that are political in nature.
There is a risk that your evidence never reaches the key individuals and teams who could use it if they knew about it.	You can ensure that your evidence has reached the key individuals and teams who need it most, and you can make sure they understand your work and its implications (even if you can't guarantee they actually act on it).
It is hard to evaluate whether or not your research had policy impacts when you were one of thousands of responses to a call for evidence.	You know who to follow up to offer future support and find out if your work was actually used and can collect evidence via a testimonial interview (see Chapter 12).
You are only able to respond to publicly available calls for evidence and may miss important opportunities to shape policy between these calls.	You gain a better understanding of policy processes that may not be in the public domain and so can proactively identify windows of opportunity where your research could be relevant.
Your research is only as accessible as you can find time to respond to calls for evidence.	By building strong, trusting relationships with key policy teams, you can potentially be available when they need help, including in a crisis.
You respect the mechanisms that are designed for researchers to engage with parliament and avoid overwhelming busy civil servants with information they don't have time to prioritise.	If your research isn't particularly important or well communicated, you may waste the time of civil servants to whom you reach out directly.
It is difficult to know how your research is being interpreted and whether or not it has been fully understood by the relevant people.	You are able to adapt to the needs, interests and questions of policy colleagues, correcting misconceptions and explaining difficult concepts, to ensure your work is as relevant and usable as possible.

experience and confidence you will need to start using some of the higher risk strategies we will outline later in this chapter.

There are many factors that will determine which of these roles will suit you best. In Figure 9.2, I have summarised how you might differentiate between seven roles on the basis of two important factors: how you view

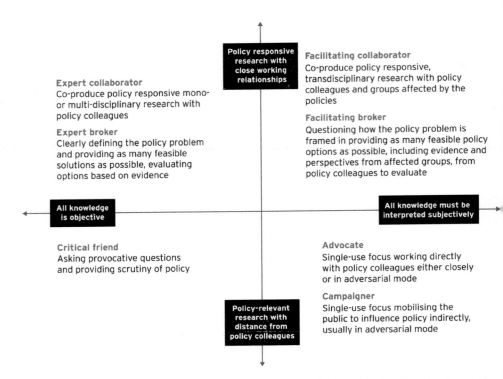

Figure 9.2 Different roles researchers can play in policy networks, based on how they view knowledge and how they view the relationship between knowledge and policy.

knowledge and how you view the relationship between knowledge and policy. There are no correct or incorrect answers, but your answers are likely to be significantly influenced by the discipline in which you were trained.

How you view knowledge, known in the social sciences as 'epistemology' influences what you consider to be valid knowledge and hence the evidence you think that should be considered in any policy decision. You might place yourself on the left side of Figure 9.2 if you see knowledge as black-and-white facts that are either right or wrong, and you see your role as generating universal, generalisable insights that can be proven objectively. On the other hand, you might place yourself further towards the right, if you see knowledge as shades of grey perspectives that could be interpreted subjectively in multiple ways by different people.

Researchers have differing views on the appropriate relationship between research and policy. Some follow the 'Haldane principle', proposed by Richard Haldane in 1918 and adapted over the years, which proposes that research should be independent of politics and free from political influence. Research can be relevant to policy but should not be driven by the political demands. To achieve this, there should be distance between researchers and policy colleagues, whether this is to remain impartial and objective or to avoid association with political decisions that conflict with the values and beliefs of the researcher. On the other hand, others argue that to achieve impact, and to remain relevant to changing policy contexts, research needs to be more responsive, adapting where possible to ensure that it delivers evidence that is useful. This requires close working relationships with policy colleagues, whether via informal engagement or formal mechanisms like project advisory boards or consultancy contracts to answer specific policy questions.

Considering these two factors can help you decide which roles you might feel most comfortable playing in policy networks. If you are already actively engaging, you will probably recognise the role or roles you tend to play, and you might start to question why you inhabit these roles and, if relevant, the reasons why you switch between different roles. If you are not yet engaging in policy networks, ask yourself which of these roles you feel most attracted to or comfortable with:

- **Critical friend:** If you view knowledge as objective and do policy-relevant research that maintains critical distance between you and your policy colleagues, then you are likely to gravitate towards the role of critical friend. I define a critical friend as someone who asks provocative questions and provides scrutiny of policy, for example by engaging directly with policy colleagues or publishing opinion pieces that question the basis of their problem framings as well as the solutions that are currently on the table, whether or not you have an alternative better solution.
- **Expert broker:** If you view knowledge as objective but want to be more responsive to policy needs, you might gravitate more towards the role of expert broker of policy options. Your role will be to clearly define the policy problem and provide as many feasible solutions as possible, evaluating each of these options, based on available evidence. You might present these options in responses to consultations and inquiries, and via policy briefs and seminars or webinars, or you might join an expert advisory group advising government or a public agency on issues related to your research.

- **Facilitating broker:** If on the other hand, you view knowledge more subjectively, you might gravitate more towards the role of a facilitating broker. I define this as someone who questions how the policy problem is framed and provides as many feasible policy options as possible, including both research evidence and perspectives from affected groups, for policy colleagues to evaluate. You might present these options in a similar way to the expert broker, but you are more likely to co-brand your policy briefs and share the stage with colleagues from outside academia.
- **Expert collaborator:** If you seek closer relationships with your policy colleagues, so you can be as responsive as possible to their needs, you may prefer to operate as a collaborator. The expert collaborator views knowledge more objectively and so is likely to rely primarily on mono- or multi-disciplinary research rather than integrating perspectives from outside academia, as they co-produce their research with policy colleagues. In addition to consultation responses, policy briefs, seminars and webinars, you may also co-author or review and advise on policy reports or co-author academic publications with policy colleagues.
- **Facilitating collaborator:** If on the other hand, you also value local knowledge and the perspectives of those who might be affected by policies as equally valid as the knowledge you generate from your research, you might be more of a facilitating collaborator. You are more likely to do transdisciplinary research that includes both your policy colleagues and groups affected by the policies in the co-production of policy options. You are likely to use similar engagement mechanisms to the expert collaborator, but you may also co-author each of these outputs with the people affected by the issues you are researching or the organisations that represent them.
- **Advocate or campaigner:** You may feel strongly about the issues you research, and although you are aware that there are opposing perspectives, you are unable to represent these vies, based on a combination of the evidence and your values. Rather than providing a dispassionate, objective comparison of different policy options, you are more likely to focus on a single problem and a particular set of solutions to that problem. If you prefer working directly with policy colleagues to make your case, whether you are working with or against the current political grain, you might describe yourself as an issue advocate. If isn't working or hasn't worked in the past for the issue you are researching

then you may move towards a campaigning role to mobilise the public and influence policy indirectly, typically in adversarial mode. Advocates use many of the same engagement mechanisms as those playing other roles, but campaigners may also use social and mass media campaigns and other ways of reaching the public, for example via debates and public dialogues. I know many researchers who are quiet advocates and hidden campaigners, providing the evidence and support to others, often in third-sector or other non-academic organisations, who work directly with policy colleagues. You can choose the extent to which you want to actually engage with the politics of the issues your research. A researcher interviewed by Justyna Bandola in her 2023 paper in *Minerva* summed this role up nicely:

> Organisations lobby all the time – drinks industry, tobacco industry – they lobby, why shouldn't we lobby? Now some of my academic colleagues feel very uncomfortable about that; they say that's a political activity and we should stay out of politics and keep our independence and we only have credibility because we are independent and we're not political. So I think there's a bid divide there about how political we should be.

Reflect on which of these roles feel most comfortable to you at this point in your career. Wherever you are comfortable at present, ask yourself if you would like to move into new roles as you develop your skills, experience and confidence. If you are more experienced in working with policy, you may wish to consider which roles you might switch between, and on what basis. You will need to balance three factors as you contemplate these different roles:

- The nature of your research and the policy challenges you seek to address;
- Your career stage and how working with policy might enhance or detract from your career goals; and
- Your personal values, confidence levels and preferences.

More objectivist approaches to research that prize independence and neutrality may be more compatible with a critical friend role, whereas more subjectivist approaches to research may enable you to switch between any of the other roles. If you work on a clearly defined issue and your evidence and/or values align with a particular set of policy options, for example around climate change or equalities, then operating as an advocate or campaigner may seem like a natural fit. If, on the other hand, you are aware of evidence for multiple alternative approaches, and prefer not to align yourself with any one of these, it may be more appropriate to work as a broker or collaborator. However, if you operate as a broker, you should be prepared not to answer or refuse to answer the inevitable question about which option you believe is best. If you work as a collaborator, you need to beware of your policy colleagues placing too much trust in you and uncritically accepting your recommendations.

Whatever your epistemology, if you are an ECR, playing the role of a critical friend might be a safe place to start, even if this limits your influence. This is because there is a degree of safety that comes with the distance between researchers and policy colleagues that is built into this role, enabling you to share knowledge without having to be interrogated publicly or asked questions that would require knowledge beyond your current expertise. As an ECR, you may prefer to spend proportionately more time building your research career because publications and research funding are typically rewarded more than impact in most academic systems, and gaining security of tenure is important. However, in doing so, you will also build your credibility in the eyes of policy colleagues, who are more likely to trust researchers with greater knowledge and experience.

But much of it is about gut feelings, which ultimately come down to your values, beliefs and preferences. If engaging in live policy settings where you will be questioned in front of large audiences terrifies you, then nobody should push you into these sorts of situations. As I confessed in Chapter 1, I regularly turn down live media opportunities because they terrify me, and that's okay. There are usually other colleagues who are delighted to make use of these opportunities. Hopefully, you will be able to think of other pitfalls and challenges associated with these different approaches as you consider which ones are the best fit for you. For example:

- If you gravitated towards informing modes of engagement in Figure 9.1 you might prioritise signing up to policy consultation email lists and following up by sending a policy brief based on your consultation response to the relevant policy team.

- If you gravitated more towards influencing, then you might want to reach out to contacts based on their interests and co-produce an impact plan. You will be more likely to want to use your policy brief in meetings where you can discuss your work, and you may want to integrate your infographics into presentations where you can engage with more people in seminars or webinars.
- If you were drawn to being a critical friend or a campaigner in Figure 9.2, you will want to use your 3i analysis to identify organisations you can work with, to hold politicians and policy teams to account. You might launch your policy brief via a press release or publish an opinion piece or open letter in a newspaper.
- If you are more of a broker, then you will want to use your 3i analysis to identify groups with different perspectives so that you can represent these alongside evidence to provide decision-makers with the widest possible range of options. You will take time to research and include options that you disagree with in your policy briefs and presentation so that decisions are based on access to the widest possible evidence base.
- If you are more of a collaborator, then you will want to take the time to co-produce your impact plan with policy colleagues and organisations in your policy networks. Your research might then feed directly into ongoing policy work or feed into the advocacy work of other organisations seeking to influence policy. You may even use your 3i analysis to build new coalitions with those who want to see the same change as you. You might consider applying for a policy shadowing scheme or fellowship, or you might bid for work being commissioned by government. You will want to co-produce policy briefs and presentations with your policy colleagues to ensure that they address relevant evidence gaps and policy needs.

Now that you appreciate whether you are aiming primarily to inform or influence, and the roles you might play to do this, the next step is to consider practical tools that can enable you to make the contacts and build the relationships necessary for you to play those roles. The first I would like to look at is the policy brief.

Part 3
Practical policy impact

CHAPTER 10

Policy briefs

The starting point for many researchers who want to influence policy is to choose a communication medium and start writing and designing their message. This is the wrong place to start. If you do not understand exactly who you are trying to communicate with, or appreciate their needs, challenges and constraints, then you are likely to blog into thin air, run policy webinars that end up being attended mainly by other academics and produce policy briefs that are never downloaded or read.

Instead, the previous chapter provided a range of tools and approaches that can enable you to gain a deep understanding of the people you need to communicate with and who might have the ability to influence the policies you want to contribute towards. Based on Chapter 8, you will have gravitated towards the sort of role you want to play in policy networks (e.g. critical friend, campaigner or collaborator), and in Chapter 9, you will have chosen an engagement strategy that can help you target the right teams and individuals in the most effective way possible. The communication tools you choose will need to be adapted to your chosen approach to working with your policy colleagues. Most of the tools I will consider in Chapters 11 and 12 can be used in any of the modes of engagement and roles I outlined in Chapter 9. The tools that follow are far from exhaustive. Instead, I have sought to consider some of the most commonly used and effective methods available, starting with policy briefs in this chapter. I have done so briefly, signposting you where possible to resources in Further Reading, as each of the methods could easily take up a book of its own, and there are many such resources already available. However, I have devoted a whole chapter to policy briefs, as many of the points about how to evidence, target and produce content for policy briefs apply to the tools covered in Chapter 11.

Each of these communication tools attempts to overcome language barriers between researchers and policy colleagues that prevent either

DOI: 10.4324/9781003494942-13

party from learning effectively from the other. Although we may each be speaking and writing in English, both researchers and policy colleagues regularly complain that they speak different languages. The problem is that one group's shortcut is jargon to another group. Policy colleagues will use acronyms and terms like 'green paper' that everyone in their networks understands, but many researchers don't know that in UK policy lingo, a green paper is effectively a discussion paper, designed to facilitate discussion of policy ideas before decisions are made. I work on ecosystem markets, but I call them 'nature markets' or 'natural capital markets' depending on whether I'm speaking to English or Scottish policy colleagues, based on the jargon they've used in their policy frameworks. However, a journal editor recently asked me to change the title of a paper I submitted to refer to them by the academic term, 'payments for ecosystem services markets' (we compromised to 'markets for ecosystem services'). Confusing as this is, I think it is important to understand and where possible use the words that are most likely to resonate with the audience we're trying to communicate with. Ultimately, we are deploying the same emotional intelligence we bring to everyday conversation, in which studies have shown we can be surprisingly adaptable, 'style shifting' to match the language and tone of the person we are speaking to.

If you want to write in a way that will be easily understood by your policy colleagues, you need to be clear on the purpose you are seeking to achieve and exactly who it is that you are seeking to communicate with. Only then can you adapt your communication to achieve your purpose with those who need to understand your research:

- Why are you trying to communicate with policy colleagues? What do you want to achieve? For example, are you providing background information, raising awareness, initiating discussion or seeking to put forward specific policy options?
- Who do you hope will engage with you or the communication products you are developing? What do you know about these people? What level of prior knowledge can you expect them to have? How much time can you expect them to give you? What issues are likely to be most relevant to their priorities?
- Based on your answers to the *why* and *who* questions, you can now ask yourself *how* you can best communicate your research. Is it better

to try and connect in-person for a two-way conversation, to use the written word, visualisations or some combination? Can you just bring a journal article along to a meeting or should you prepare a slide deck or policy brief you can present or leave with them? How technical should these materials be, and should you keep it as short and visual as possible for high-level decision-makers or provide more detail to help analysts with their job?

In the rest of this chapter, I will try and answer these questions in the context of writing policy briefs, but many of the lessons apply equally to writing opinion pieces in the mass media, infographics and visualisations, slide decks and giving testimony to inquiries and committees. In each case, you will have to make your own judgements on the 'why' and 'who' questions, to adapt this more generic advice to your purpose and audience.

WHAT MAKES A GOOD POLICY BRIEF?

For researchers, a policy brief should be: i) a short summary or synthesis of research evidence that ii) clearly targets an issue, evidence gap or policy need; iii) communicates complexity and uncertainty responsibly; iv) provides technically and politically feasible policy options or questions existing options to open up new opportunity spaces; and v) is never developed in isolation. In reality, most policy briefs do not conform to all four of these suggestions, so this section will explore the pitfalls and challenges in each of these areas, alongside practical strategies for including each one effectively.

A good policy brief summarises or syntheses evidence

It might seem obvious that a policy brief should be evidence-based, but policy briefs from think tanks and interest groups are often based around new ideas rather than evidence. Although policy briefs produced by researchers, universities and research funders typically contain research evidence, more often than not, they focus on the work of an individual researcher, project or funding programme, to the exclusion of other potentially important evidence. This is an important problem for a number of reasons. First, the policy options might not be sufficiently robust, and so might lead to unintended consequences. If the evidence base for a policy intervention is mixed or inconclusive, a clear finding from a single new study does not change the nature of the evidence base overall; there are still multiple studies with findings that contradict yours as well as those that point in the same direction as your new study. You need to understand the basis for these contradictions in the evidence base, ideally using meta-analysis methods to disentangle the apparently contradictory evidence before you can say anything with certainty. Another common challenge is over-extrapolation of findings to the jurisdictional scales at which policies operate. The findings may be of national and international significance to other academics who might want to build on your research. However, care must be taken when discussing implications for policy and practice in your research, unless there is strong evidence that your conclusions really do apply across the many diverse contexts that will be found at any jurisdictional scale. Second, poorly evidenced policy briefs undermine trust in the research community. If your policy brief makes bold claims that a policy analyst later discovers are contested in the majority of the peer-reviewed literature, they could be forgiven for doubting your motives. In reality, you were probably asked to focus on your own project by the funder who asked you to write the policy brief, and/or you didn't have time to put your research into a broader context. However, the audience for your policy brief is unlikely to be aware of these mitigating circumstances.

The solution is to either summarise or synthesise the broader evidence base as part of your policy brief. There are three approaches you can take, increasing in the amount of time and effort they take:

1. **Summarise key findings from the broader evidence base using narrative literature review methods** and distil the key points to provide a concise summary in your policy brief (consider using the method described in *The Productive Researcher* so you can complete this in around one to two days - see Further Reading). A brief narrative review is appropriate for evidence that cannot be considered in terms of discrete interventions or options that lead to specific outcomes that can be compared between studies. It is also useful when there are very different ways of framing or researching an issue in the published literature that cannot legitimately be compared, for example quantitative

statistical studies that provide precise estimates versus qualitative studies that examine the assumptions underpinning statistical models to suggest these figures might be very precise but inaccurate or simply a partial or skewed representation of the issue.

2. **Conduct a Rapid Evidence Synthesis, if possible including meta-analysis**, summarising your findings as the basis for the policy options you suggest, potentially including a case study based on your project or publication. See Chapter 7 and Further Reading for more on these methods. It is possible to write a Rapid Review in one week from beginning to end (that's how long the residential synthesis writing workshops I ran with Gav Stewart took, which I mentioned in Chapter 7), but most people would reserve a month for this task, assuming they could devote the majority of that time to the review. A Rapid Review that went into a policy brief I wrote recently was done by four researchers working in parallel over the course of three months, alongside their other duties. Figure 10.1 shows the front page and one of the inner pages showing the results of a rapid review that my colleagues and I did to inform the design of post-Brexit agri-environment schemes.

3. **Integrate evidence across a complex system to evaluate or simulate likely policy outcomes in uncertain and complex policy contexts.** There is a range of tools available for this. Although there is not space here to describe each in detail, there are three categories. First, there are qualitative and heuristic methods (e.g. the integration of different sources of evidence in narrative scenarios, logic maps that provide a conceptual model of the system and how policy options are likely to play out or the creation of a decision support system based on evidence). Second, you might consider modelling methods (e.g. process-based, computation models, leading to predictions with clear statements around uncertainty, for example expressed as scenarios with sensitivity analysis). Finally, there are mixed methods approaches that can combine qualitative and quantitative data sources with models and expert opinion (e.g. dynamic systems models and Bayesian networks, which show how evidence pertaining to different system components and relationships between components might interact to produce policy outcomes). For example, I recently wrote a policy brief based on this sort of evidence, which arose from a four-month project that included both Rapid Reviews and the creation of a Bayesian Network. The model

What is the evidence that public money leads to public goods delivery from agri-environment schemes?

Key messages

- There is strong evidence that public goods including climate change mitigation, improved water quality and soil health can be provided by several on-farm interventions, such as watercourse fencing to exclude livestock, conservation tillage and planting hedges in arable land

- However, for the majority of options and public goods investigated, evidence was mixed or weak, and it was not possible to assess the magnitude or rate of change, requiring more research

- There are policy options that could prioritise public money for public goods that can most reliably be delivered, while developing the evidence-base for interventions that are feasible on-farm via Environmental Land Management Scheme (ELMS) pilot trials

(a)

Figure 10.1 Example of how evidence synthesis can be used to inform the content of a policy brief (the [a] first and [b] second pages are shown; for the full brief visit the Resilient Dairy Landscapes project website). *(Continued)*

The Research

Researchers have assessed the evidence base for a number of agri-environment options, asking whether they deliver on 'public money for public goods'. Two teams of researchers completed reviews of 13 options, considering evidence from over 250 peer-reviewed papers:

- Options consider included: fencing waterways from livestock, soil loosening, tree planting on floodplains, conversion of grass to woodland or arable to woodland, buffer strips, agroforestry, conservation tillage, organic amendments to arable land, hedges, cover crops, over-winter stubble and leys in arable rotations

- Public goods evaluated were: water quality (including N and P concentrations, suspended sediment, E. coli), flood risk alleviation (based on changes in channel discharge, soil bulk density, aggregate stability, porosity, infiltration rate and hydraulic conductivity), climate change mitigation (carbon stocks) and soil health (based on eight soil health indicators)

The research was conducted by the Resilient Dairy Landscapes project and Yorkshire Integrated Catchment Solutions Programme (see further information

Key Findings

The following table lists agri-environment options for which there was robust evidence for specific public goods, based on certain well-studied indicators.

For other options and public goods, evidence was mixed or weak and it was not possible to assess the magnitude or rate of change, requiring more research. For

example, planting trees on floodplains reduces channel discharge[1], but the effect was variable[2], the potential for confounding was high, and publication bias is strongly suspected[3]. Due to the lack of direct evidence the overall strength of evidence is low, indicating high uncertainty.

Scheme option	Public good (indicator used in brackets)
Watercourse fencing to exclude livestock	Water quality (led to a reduction in P and E. Coli)
Converting arable land to woodland	Climate change mitigation (soil carbon stock increases)
Grass-clover leys in arable rotation	Climate change mitigation (soil carbon increases)
Conservation tillage	Soil health (soil carbon, aggregate stability, infiltration all increase)
Hedges in arable land	Climate change mitigation (soil carbon increases)
Organic amendments	Climate (soil carbon increases) and soil health (aggregate stability, earthworms) BUT could lead to reductions in water quality if the amendment contains high concentrations of nutrients, heavy metals, pathogens and emerging contaminates

[1] Standardised mean difference -0.35, 95%CI, -0.71 to 0.00
[2] I^2 = 81.91%
[3] Egger Test z = 3.0568, p = 0.002

(b)

Figure 10.1 (Continued)

was able to identify key risks arising from Brexit that might need to be managed, and the review identified a number of policy options being pursued by other countries facing similar problems that could be relevant to the UK.

A good policy brief communicates complexity and uncertainty responsibly

Based on the methods above, it is highly likely that the evidence you want to communicate will come with a number of caveats and uncertainties. These may arise from the methods or assumptions underpinning your research, the interpretation of findings, the unknown ways in which target populations might respond or unknown interactions between policy interventions when they are applied in combination or in new untested contexts. You also have to factor in the complexity and inherent unpredictability of policymakers themselves, who may be vulnerable to interpreting your findings in ways that are biased, for example based on stereotyped assumptions about a target population, a stronger aversion to losses than appreciation of gains or unrealistic hopes for policies that have already received significant investment, leading to policy lock-in where 'good money is thrown after bad'.

You will therefore need to think carefully about how to represent these complexities in a way that your audience will appreciate:

- In some cases, uncertainty may be represented statistically to show the probability of different outcomes. You might then use probabilistic language to express uncertainty, for example using phrases like 'there is a 70% chance' of a particular outcome, or by using phrases to represent probability ranges such as 'highly likely' to represent a probability of over 70%.
- In other cases, you may need to draw on theories of human behaviour to try and evaluate how different target populations are likely to respond to a policy intervention and hence identify potential unintended consequences. These may be modelled or represented statistically for example using social network analysis or agent-based models. However, it is more likely that you will use theories to identify potential challenges that may need to be managed. For example, we might

question the assumptions behind a new subsidy regime that is designed to drive sustainable farming practices, on the basis that we know that farmer behaviour is also influenced by values, beliefs, social norms and culture and that older, less formally educated farmers are less likely to try new farming practices.

- Where other governments in comparable contexts have applied a policy option, you might be able to draw on a range of experiences to show how the application of that policy option might work out in the context in which you are proposing it.

- One way of communicating this range of outcomes from a given policy option is by using scenarios. In some cases, these will be modelled statistically. For example, Box 10.1 shows how a model was developed by University of Bristol researchers to enable policymakers to evaluate different vaccination scenarios, leading health departments in three countries to introduce a new vaccine. These kinds of scenario studies can integrate sensitivity analysis to identify key factors that have a significant impact on the outcomes, which might then become a focus for future policy. Scenarios may be more heuristic, building a credible story that explains how a policy option might have different consequences depending on a range of factors you have identified from theory and practice. I regularly integrate insights from qualitative research with scenarios that also include model outputs and insights from academic literature. Scenarios may be supported by visualisations to help communicate complexity as clearly as possible, although as I will explain in the next chapter, this has to be done carefully to avoid creating biases and misunderstanding.

Box 10.1 Using model-based scenarios to influence vaccination policy.

Hannah Christensen and colleagues from University of Bristol developed models that integrated epidemiological and economic data to predict the potential impact of introducing a new meningococcal vaccine that would protect people against the Meningococcal B strain of the disease.

They used their models to consider different MenB vaccine scenarios, showing which vaccine strategy could avert the most cases most cost-effectively. These scenarios informed a decision by the Department of Health to introduce the Bexsero vaccine against group MenB for babies in 2015, and MenB cases had been reduced by 75% by the third year of the programme. The research has also informed vaccination policy in Belgium and Germany.

A good policy brief is clearly targeted

The second component of an effective policy brief is that it clearly targets a policy need, challenge or policy-relevant evidence gap. The temptation is to start a policy brief by looking at your research (or perhaps better, by looking at the broader evidence base in the area you are researching). However, a better starting point is understanding the policy challenges being faced by people in relevant policy networks. The only way to do this is to identify relevant people who are either directly working on policy or who are indirectly working with those involved in the policy process, so you can ask them what the most important questions are that you need to try and answer in your policy brief. You may discover that you do not have answers to the questions that really matter, but it is better to discover this and initiate a collaboration with someone who might have more relevant evidence at their fingertips than it is to plough on with your original idea when you know nobody will be interested.

Part of this step is about fine-graining your focus. You may be aware of the broad policy area, but within that broad area, there will be particular issues that need to be urgently resolved, depending on the programme of legislation and political drivers. Without understanding these nuances, you could produce something generally relevant that is not specifically relevant to any individual team or policy process and so gets ignored.

It is important to consider who you speak to, as you seek to better understand and frame the problem you aim to address in your advice. Politicians with different ideologies might frame the issue very differently to each other, and agency staff working on the front line might see the issue very differently to civil servants working in a government department. The organisations and groups that they ultimately hope to help may in turn see the issue very differently again. For example, the issue I studied for my PhD was framed by the Government of Botswana as an economic problem: how to modernise agriculture to generate more beef exports (which at the time were second only to diamonds in the export economy). As a natural scientist, my supervisor had reframed the issue as an environmental issue where the government's policy of privatising communal rangeland was leading to communal herds being concentrated in ever smaller areas, leading to land degradation. If, on the other hand, you spoke to the affected communities, they would have reframed the policy problem as a social issue where current policies were widening the gap between rich and poor and threatening the livelihoods of the poorest and most marginalised groups in society. In supposedly democratic systems around the world, policy problems are typically framed by the most powerful people in society, including researchers, often disregarding the perspectives of local people as just that - perspectives not evidence.

As such, part of the researcher's task is to think critically about how a policy problem has been framed to them by members of policy teams, who may themselves be unaware of biases in their own framing of the issue. In some cases, however, these perspectives may have been shaped by lobbyists who have purposefully attempted to frame an issue in a way that will benefit their interests while compromising the interests of other, less powerful actors. As a result, Paul Cairney, in his 2021 book *The Politics of Policy Analysis*, suggests that researchers themselves need to become more influential in framing and reframing policy issues in ways that reflect a wider constituency of interests, while also reflecting on their own biases.

A good policy brief identifies technically and politically feasible actions or questions existing options to open up new opportunity spaces

The third component of an effective policy brief is that it provides policy options, advice or actions that could deliver benefits to society. Unlike policy briefs, briefing notes (like POSTnotes in UK Parliament) may seek to provide thematic overviews of research in a general area, providing no concrete suggestions for policy. However, a policy brief that seeks to inform and influence policy needs to provide guidance to the reader in the form of options or actions that they might take, based on the evidence you have presented. I tend to steer away from the word 'recommendations' these days, as this implies that the researcher knows best, when in reality the decision will be partly political, drawing on many other sources of information. The challenge is to create policy options that are both technically and politically feasible. There is no point proposing a politically acceptable option that is not technically possible to deliver, and there is no point in proposing something that is technically feasible that would instantly cause public uproar. To assess the acceptability of policy options, consider how different types of policy actors (from civil servants to politicians), implementers, target populations and other relevant parties are likely to react, possibly using a 3i analysis (see Chapter 5). Alternatively, you might use criteria such as efficiency, equity and fairness, trade-offs between individual freedom and collective action, the extent to which a policy involves relevant parties in deliberation and the likely impact on a policymaker's popularity (you can choose for yourself which of these you think are valid and appropriate). Some policy briefs make these criteria explicit by comparing key policy options against each other in a table, where policy options are described in rows and each criterion is given a column, where considerations (such as efficiency versus equity) are taken into account in turn for each policy option (for more on this, see the multicriteria evaluation methods in my *Research Impact Handbook*).

While you may wish to propose policy options that are not likely to be acceptable at the present time, it is worth understanding the reasons why your option is not likely to be accepted and make interim suggestions around actions that might increase the acceptability of your ideas, for example via public information campaigns. There are some policy options that, despite limited feasibility in the short term, are too important to ignore, for example gender mainstreaming or action to address climate change, and we should not shy away from presenting evidence that shows the importance of addressing such issues. However, we may want to invest more time and resources in researching solutions to these issues rather than just further evidencing the magnitude of the problem, in order to start presenting well-evidenced potential solutions.

Depending on the mode of engagement and role you feel most comfortable occupying in your policy networks, you may prefer, instead of identifying actionable policy options, to question the basis of existing options being considered. Even if you do not have better alternatives, it is still useful to use evidence in this way, as it may prevent negative unintended consequences and open up new opportunity spaces in which alternative approaches could be developed. I have found this a surprisingly rewarding way to work with policy colleagues. For example, a few years ago, I managed to get access to an early draft of a new policy strategy through my policy networks and could instantly see that one of their key ideas was not only unlikely to work in practice but also, based on my understanding of the literature, it could lead to significant unintended negative consequences that could undermine the goals of the strategy. As soon as I pointed out the flaw in their logic, the policy lead for the strategy realised that they would have to change tack, and she asked me how to fix the problem I had identified. Sadly, I explained to her that I had no idea. All I knew was that the current plan was unlikely to work. However, she commissioned some new research, and happily others with bigger brains than me were able to come up with some alternatives, which were subsequently integrated into the strategy.

Recently, a number of third-sector organisations have started to lobby against the policy options I have been advocating for, based on my research. Their goal has been to question the political basis and assumptions underpinning these policy options, in an attempt to open up space for very different sorts of solutions, which they believe will avoid some of the negative unintended consequences of the current approach, which are beginning to become apparent. By engaging with their work, I have come to realise that I fell victim to the same assumptions that my policy colleagues were making, namely that capitalism is here to stay, and we have to work within the capitalist model to tackle climate change. This is despite the self-evident reality that the climate crisis has been driven by capitalism and the growing evidence that investment in carbon offsetting is enabling fossil fuel giants to greenwash their way to a social licence to continue operating as they have always done. Furthermore, the markets I helped create have started pushing people off the land to make way for forests across Scotland, in what author and political commentator Alistair MacIntosh has described as 'carbon clearances'. As a member of the Just Transition Commission, advising Scottish Government on how it can meet its net zero targets without leaving anyone behind, I have heard from local communities, tenants and crofters who stand to lose much but gain little from these new markets. Instead, my third-sector colleagues are pointing out that the need for private finance to tackle climate change has in fact been driven by political decisions not to allocate public funding or introduce new taxes that could tackle the crisis without having to rely on private finance. Despite sitting on the Executive Board of the Peatland Code and being on teams setting up new carbon markets for saltmarsh restoration, agroforestry and regenerative agriculture, I am now collaborating with these colleagues to open up debate and encourage our policy colleagues to think more critically about the role that the public sector might play and how they might better regulate private investment in these markets.

A good policy brief is never developed in isolation

A powerful way of evaluating the political feasibility of options and questioning your own assumptions, while also better targeting a policy challenge or evidence gap, is to get feedback on your policy brief from members of relevant policy networks. This might take the form of verbal feedback from one or two members of a relevant policy team or written feedback from an academic colleague who is actively engaged with that team. In some cases, I have taken this further, to actually co-produce the policy brief with relevant policy colleagues, especially in projects commissioned by policy bodies. In this case, the starting point is typically a question from a policy team, whether informally via your networks or more formally, for example linked to consultation questions or commissioned research (see Figure 10.2 for the first page of a policy brief created in Microsoft Word by an academic, based on a consultation response they had submitted to government). You will co-construct the problem framing with your policy colleagues, who may identify particular policy options they would like you to research as part of the process of developing the brief. They will also give you constructive feedback on drafts. What makes this approach so powerful is that the policy teams have a far more intimate understanding of your research and the policy options you have presented because they have had to engage so deeply with the process of developing the policy brief. Also, given their investment in the process they are more likely to send the policy brief to other colleagues internally who in turn are more likely to engage with the policy brief if they trust their colleagues' judgement and therefore trust that it will be worth their time engaging with your work.

In addition, you might stress-test your policy brief by sending it to groups who you think are likely to hold opposing views on the issue you are targeting. This can be particularly useful for policy briefs or controversial topics. The feedback you receive might highlight important missing points or evidence you were unaware of or provide a perspective that you might want to incorporate or challenge directly in your brief. It is better to identify challenges via a review process like this than it is to identify them in a live policy scenario, say during questions at a policy seminar. In some cases, certain groups will be opposed to the messages in your policy brief for ideological reasons. While you are unlikely to

Women's Health Strategy, Consultation Response

WRITTEN EVIDENCE

Accessibility of information and quality of evidence in the fertility sector

KEY FINDINGS

• Our research shows that there is a lot of information available about infertility and fertility treatments, including conflicting information on the evidence available to support additional treatments (add-ons)

• This abundance of information provision can be difficult to navigate and identifying good quality information can be challenging

• Women undergoing or preparing for fertility treatment will generally undertake substantial online research into treatment options

• Google search, fertility clinic websites and social media emerged as particularly important sources of information

• Women often described difficulties in finding up-to-date and geographically specific information about how to access fertility treatment in their area

• Women sometimes found it difficult to understand the available information about IVF treatment add-ons and do not always feel equipped to evaluate their effectiveness

• Many women did not know that the Human Fertilisation and Embryology Authority website provides information about add-ons specifically for patients

• There is no consensus in the medical community on how to assess evidence and what sort of evidence should be considered when evaluating IVF treatment add-ons

• Professionals and patients understand evidence in different ways and this has a potential impact on the quality of care

FURTHER CONTRIBUTION

As our study focuses on reproduction, we would be interested in making further contributions to the next open consultation on reproductive health

This submission responds to the government's development of a Women's Health Strategy drawing on the findings from empirical research with fertility patients and their partners as well as fertility professionals. Focusing on in vitro fertilisation (IVF) in particular, this document addresses core themes Two (the quality and accessibility of information) and Five (how evidence is used in medical practice) as stated in the call for evidence. We believe this consultation presents an opportunity to dramatically improve the experience of IVF patients.

The research, based at Queen Mary University of London and funded by the Wellcome Trust, is unique in its ability to provide insights both into the perspectives of professionals who provide fertility treatment and patients/partners' experiences of receiving fertility treatment. The geographical focus of the study is England.

POLICY IMPLICATIONS

• Women need a more coordinated provision of up-to-date information about IVF, especially information about novel IVF treatment add-ons

• Improving the clarity, visibility and accessibility of already available information is a relatively low-cost measure that will bring timely positive change for IVF patients

• There is an opportunity for the NHS A-Z website to direct IVF patients to the Human Fertilisation and Embryology Authority's website for information specifically about new IVF treatment add-ons

• Different understandings of evidence should be considered to improve the quality of information on new treatment add-ons

• Accurate information about the nature of available evidence should be provided when treatment add-ons are experimental

Dr Manuela Perrotta and Dr Josie Hamper

Department of People and Organisations
School of Business and Management
Faculty of Humanities and Social Sciences
Queen Mary University of London

Figure 10.2 Example of a policy brief created using PowerPoint by Dr Manuela Perrotta and Dr Josie Hamper, based on a response they had made to a policy consultation.

want to change your brief in response to such feedback, it can be useful to flush out arguments that may later be used to undermine or delegitimise your work and be prepared for political questions from these perspectives in live policy settings like workshops, media interviews and policy conferences.

The messiness of these more engaged approaches to policy brief development isn't always straightforward, however. Once, a Professor on one of my projects demanded my resignation as Principal Investigator, after I attempted to rush a stress-testing process. This happened in the lead up to the closed doors debate with the President of the National Farmers Union, which I described in Chapter 7. To ensure my position was solid, I asked my research team to work with me to write a policy brief that I could take to London with me. However, some members of the team were unhappy with the amount of time we had to do the work. To make matters worse, I was then invited to appear on the UK's most popular breakfast television show, which had an audience of 2 million, to debate the issue ahead of the debate, further shortening our deadline. I regretted agreeing to the appearance almost immediately, as the complaints from my team grew louder and I started to worry that my debating skills were not up to the job. I barely slept the night before the appearance, which involved a particularly early rise, as they had transported the red sofa that their show was famous for using to host its guests, halfway up a mountainside for the debate, which was about the future of the country's uplands. The debate went surprisingly well. What I hadn't expected was the reaction of my team to my appearance. I returned home, sleep deprived, to an angry email from one of my colleagues, who was demanding my resignation because I had brought him and the rest of the team into disrepute. He was a climate modeller and took an objectivist approach to his research and typically engaged with policy colleagues as a critical friend. In contrast, was an environmental social scientist, taking a more subjectivist approach to my research and engaging as a 'facilitating influencer' (see Figure 9.1, in the role of facilitating collaborator and broker, at the time. He had two principal objections. First, as he saw it, I had changed the facts. His second objection, as a conservationist and climate campaigner who believed that farmers were largely responsible for climate change and biodiversity loss, was that I had given his opponents evidence that we had changed our story, which they could use against us to discredit us as researchers

During the stress-testing process, I realised that all the objections centred on what would happen to sheep in the uplands after Brexit, which was a distraction to the ultimate impacts on climate change and biodiversity resulting from changes in numbers of sheep. I therefore reframed the briefing from an initial framing around what will happen if there are no more sheep in the uplands to how changes in upland management, including sheep numbers, might affect the carbon and biodiversity held in these landscapes. The evidence remained the same, but the way it was framed would avoid attention being diverted to whether people love or hate sheep, to the issues that the evidence was ultimately pointing to. However, if there is such a thing as objective truth, then it shouldn't be possible to rewrite a policy brief in this way; if facts are facts, then there can only be the facts, and you can't rewrite them. Ultimately, after a long conversation about epistemology, my colleague backed down and I kept my job. But the process of stress-testing the policy brief had been worth it. It had enabled me to flush out all the arguments I subsequently faced in debate, which I was able to prepare for. The policy brief was also more robust as a result. In addition to this, some of the people we sent it to had pointed us to important evidence that we had missed (we didn't have time to do a systematic review of the literature). Not only did this further strengthen our policy brief and arguments for the debate but also it was far preferable to learn about these crucial pieces of evidence ahead of time rather than being caught off-guard by new evidence in front of a policy audience.

DESIGNING YOUR POLICY BRIEF

You can design your own policy brief using software like Microsoft Word or PowerPoint, or you can pitch your work into a policy brief series, if one exists for your research area or your institution has an existing policy brief template. If you are designing your own policy brief, you may want to get professional help with your design, and you will need to make sure you have permission to use any logos you want to include on it. Design matters because readers will subconsciously associate shoddy, unprofessional design with untrustworthy information. Most readers do not have time to look up your CV and decide whether or not you are trustworthy, relying instead on proxies for trust such as the logos that appear on the front or back of your policy brief and their design.

However, if you do not have the budget to work with a professional designer, there are a few things you can do yourself to make sure your design looks as professional as possible. For example:

- Use a limited colour palette (between one and three colours) and consider matching this to logos or the photo you have chosen for the front page avoid clashing colours. Do some research on complementary colours and get feedback on your choice of colours. Different people will pick on different issues, for example a black, orange and red colour scheme might remind people of fire safety posters (red is often interpreted as a warning or danger, and so is a colour I would try and avoid). When choosing colours, think about accessibility for people who are colour blind or who need strong contrast to be able to read text easily.
- Keep text to a minimum on your front page and throughout your policy brief. Being confronted with big blocks of text (especially on the front page) is off-putting to readers. Where you have significant amounts of text, always try and reduce the length first, before breaking up the remaining text with short paragraphs, bullet lists, images, diagrams, boxes, subheadings, infographics and blank space. Blank space is important to draw a reader in. Even if you have lots of graphics, if everything is crammed together on the page, it will look busy and confusing. Use lots of subheadings to signpost your key points, making the subheadings sufficiently informative that someone skim reading the brief is able to pick up the key points from them.
- Include an image or infographic on the front page that will catch people's attention and help communicate your key messages powerfully.
- Consider placing your university and/or funder logos on the front page (with permission) to add provenance and weight to your message.

STRUCTURING YOUR CONTENT

How you structure your content also matters, starting with your front page. Include a concise and prominent title that instantly anchors your policy brief in a relevant policy area using relevant keywords that resonate with your target audience. Make sure the title tells the reader exactly what they will get by reading your policy brief. If you can't do that easily enough in the title, keep your title short and eye-catching and write a strapline underneath, to explain more fully what they will get if they read on. I quite like policy brief titles that are questions, as long as you are sure that the question is something your audience wants an answer to. You might then summarise your answer to the question in a strapline underneath the question, to interest the reader in what follows.

In addition to any images or graphics that are designed to catch the reader's attention, it is important to include a box with key policy messages or options somewhere on the front page. These should be specific and actionable, if possible, making it clear why they are both technically and politically feasible. However, the text should be concise to avoid cluttering up your front page, so avoid too much detail, which can be provided in the main body of the policy brief. Alternatively, if you can communicate this clearly enough with your title and strapline, you might want to put these messages clearly on the back page.

The back page of a policy brief can be used for a number of different things. If you are printing copies, bear in mind that busy people may only read the front and back page, so you might want to do more than just include your references on your last page. Some policy briefs include references in footnotes, so the majority of the back page can be used for something else, for example information about your project or funder or key messages for other audiences (such as delivery agencies or practitioners). As an alternative to references, you might include a 'Further Reading' or 'Find Out More' section on your back pages with key publications or a link to a webpage with multiple relevant publications. It is important that somewhere on the back page, you include your contact details. You may also want to put your logos on the back page rather than the front page, if leaving them on the front page will make your design look too busy.

For the inside pages, a common structure is to start first with the challenges for policy that need to be addressed (this can include some wider contextual points that are essential for readers to understand what follows). The second section will typically focus on the research, summarising methods or any other information that will help the reader evaluate the trustworthiness of the findings you are presenting (this may include evidence gaps and limitations). Remember where possible to try and include an element of evidence synthesis rather than just focusing on single studies, perhaps focusing on the wider body of work, followed by a box with examples and details from your project. Third and finally, you will want to expand on the policy options and/or messages you alluded to on the front page, drawing on your evidence to justify each point, highlighting uncertainties and potential issues as you go. This would normally include a critical appraisal of the policy options, possibly comparing options against each other or against relevant criteria (e.g. efficiency versus equity), and may in some cases conclude with a preferred option on the basis of the evidence.

Policy jargon is okay and in some cases might be beneficial if it helps anchor your work in a specific policy area, but avoid academic jargon where possible, defining terms where this is absolutely necessary. Tools like the Up-Goer Six text editor (https://splasho.com/upgoer6/) are useful to help you identify words that might be jargon. Alternatively, you might use generative artificial intelligence to make suggestions for plain English versions of particularly jargonised sentences. You can also employ an editor and/or proof-reader to help with this (you can hire these yourself online if there is nobody available in your institution to help).

Although most policy briefs are between four and eight pages long, some are just one side of A4 and some are much longer. This is not necessarily a problem, depending on the target audience. For evidence analysts and those in policy networks whose task it is to translate evidence into policy, a longer and more technical policy brief may be more useful than a very short, high-level summary. However, for politicians and senior decision-makers, shorter, simpler policy briefs are better, making more use of infographics.

In Figure 10.3, you can see how the large headline immediately anchors the policy brief in an important current policy area (childhood food poverty) with an arresting image that catches the eye and complements the title. The University of Leeds logo is prominent, giving provenance and weight to the document. The design is simple, using a graphic from Policy Leeds in the corner of each page of the policy brief, with titles chosen from a limited palette that matches the blue from this graphic. The overview provides a summary of the research and the key policy messages. On the back page, recommendations are divided into two different sets, each targeting a different policy community. These are made prominent using an orange box (matching the boxes used on the

Policy
Leeds

UNIVERSITY OF LEEDS

Tackling childhood food poverty in the UK

Brief 4
09 Dec 2020
Policy Leeds
University of Leeds
leeds.ac.uk/policy-leeds

Bernadette Moore and Charlotte Evans

Actions are needed from national government and local authorities to reduce reliance on emergency food provision, improve take-up of eligible financial support, and develop sustainable food system resilience in diverse communities. Reducing childhood poverty brings life-long benefits to health and wellbeing with economic benefits to society.

Overview

- A panel of experts was convened to examine current efforts aimed at mitigating childhood food poverty.

- Childhood food poverty leads to poor health and educational outcomes. Families and the wider social context early in childhood must be considered.

- Cost-benefit analyses show positive economic and social benefits to early years interventions and reducing childhood and adolescent hunger.

- Implementation of the recommendations from the National Food Strategy to expand eligibility for free school meals including breakfast will narrow inequalities in health and educational attainment.

- Local authorities need to increase access to high quality, affordable food alongside offering programmes that empower families in diverse communities to live independently with dignity.

Policy context

In 2019 an estimated 30%, or 4.2 million, of children in the UK were living in poverty[1]. This number has increased steadily over the last 10 years alongside a rise in childhood obesity. The COVID-19 pandemic has led to a quadrupling of food insecurity in families, increasing applications for free school meals and the use of foodbanks and food charities. The National Food Strategy, released in July 2020, made several recommendations to mitigate childhood food poverty[2]. With the footballer Marcus Rashford championing this issue, the Government's COVID Winter Grant Scheme and decisions to increase Healthy Start payments and extend the Holiday Activities and Food programme through

(a)

Figure 10.3 Example policy brief using the Policy Leeds PowerPoint template (showing the [a] first and [b] last pages only; the full text is available on the Policy Leeds website) (this work is licensed under Creative Commons, CC-BY 4.0). *(Continued)*

Recommendations

National

- Implementation of all the recommendations from the National Food Strategy
- More financial support for local authorities for measuring food insecurity, improving food access, and increasing food resilience and sustainability
- Increase in family-centred support focussed on increasing household income to empower families to live independently

Local authorities

- Prioritise early start interventions that foster healthy pregnancies and healthy food and lifestyle behaviours in young families
- Increase access to high quality & affordable housing
- Increase access to campaigns offering clear information on rules surrounding housing and benefits eligibility and empower people back to work
- Target funding to primary and secondary schools for schemes such as free school breakfasts, or those that imbed sustainable solutions such as redistributing surplus food to Schools

About the authors

Bernadette Moore is Associate Professor at the University of Leeds. She is an expert in obesity related metabolic disease and leads the Nutritional Sciences and Epidemiology Research Group in the School of Food Science and Nutrition.
Telephone: +44(0)113 343 9900
Email: J.B.Moore@leeds.ac.uk

Charlotte Evans is Associate Professor of Nutritional Epidemiology and Public Health at the University of Leeds, researching the importance of school food on diet and health.
Telephone: +44(0)113 343 3956
Email: C.E.L.Evans@leeds.ac.uk

The authors would like to gratefully acknowledge and thank the members of the panel for critically reviewing this brief.

Further information

A recording of the N8 AgriFood panel discussion that informed this brief is available at: https://policyhub.n8agrifood.ac.uk/launch-week/childhood-food-poverty/

References

1. Moore JB & Evans CEL (2020) Obese and hungry: two faces of a nation. BMJ 370 https://doi.org/10.1136/bmj.m3084

2. Dimbleby H (2020) National Food Strategy: Part One https://www.nationalfoodstrategy.org/wp-content/uploads/2020/07/NFS-Part-One-SP-CP.pdf

3. Evans C, Hutchinson J, Christian M, Hancock N & Cade JE (2018) Measures of low food variety and poor dietary quality in a cross-sectional study of London school children. Eur J Clin Nutr https://doi.org/10.1038/s41430-017-0070-1

4. Willis TA, Roberts KP, Berry TM, Bryant M & Rudolf MC (2016) The impact of HENRY on parenting and family lifestyle: A national service evaluation of a preschool obesity prevention programme. Public Health https://doi.org/10.1016/j.puhe.2016.04.006

5. Bramley G, Hirsch D, Littlewood M & Watkins D (2016) Counting the cost of UK poverty. Joseph Rowntree Foundation https://www.jrf.org.uk/report/counting-cost-uk-poverty

6. Greater London Authority Economics (2011) Early Years Interventions to address Health Inequalities in London –The Economic Case. https://www.london.gov.uk/what-we-do/health/health-publications/early-years-interventions-address-health-inequalities-london

7. Adolphus K, Lawton C & Dye L (2013) The effects of breakfast on behavior and academic performance in children and adolescents. Front Hum Neurosci https://doi.org/10.3389/fnhum.2013.00425

8. Adolphus K, Lawton C & Dye L (2019) Associations Between Habitual School-Day Breakfast Consumption Frequency and Academic Performance in British Adolescents. Front Public Health https://doi.org/10.3389/fpubh.2019.00283

9. Farquharson C (2020) No free lunch? Some pros and cons of holiday free school meals. Institute for Fiscal Studies https://www.ifs.org.uk/publications/15148

10. Tucker J (2017) The Austerity Generation: the impact of a decade of cuts on family incomes and child poverty. Child Poverty Action Group. https://cpag.org.uk/sites/default/files/files/Austerity%20Generation%20FINAL.pdf

11. Blake MK (2019) More than Just Food: Food Insecurity and Resilient Place Making through Community Self-Organising. Sustainability https://doi.org/10.3390/su11102942

12. Graven C, Power M, Jones S, Possingham S & Bryant M (2020) Interim Report: The impact of COVID-19 on the provision of food aid in Bradford. https://www.bradfordresearch.nhs.uk/wp-content/uploads/2020/11/Maria-Bryant-Interim-Report_CFA.pdf

13. Patterson G & Rushton J (2020) Food Access for All: Overcoming Barriers to Food Access in the Liverpool City Region. Policy Brief 015 https://www.liverpool.ac.uk/media/livacuk/publicpolicyamppractice/covid-19/PB015.pdf

UNIVERSITY OF LEEDS

Tel. +44 (0)113 2431751
policyleeds@leeds.ac.uk
leeds.ac.uk/policy-leeds
@policyleeds

N8 AgriFood
**Food Systems
Policy Hub**

firstlove
FOUNDATION

h❤nry

Policy Leeds
University of Leeds
Leeds, United Kingdom LS2 9JT

(b)

Figure 10.3 *(Continued)*

inside pages), which complements the blue and picks up the orange from the graphic in the top left corner. In addition to the references used in the policy brief (which have been kept to a minimum), you can follow up to find out more about the researchers, their work and the programme that funded them. More details of the research and policy options are provided in the inner two pages.

DIFFERENT WAYS TO USE YOUR POLICY BRIEF

It is important to consider how you will use your policy brief. There is an almost magical belief among some researchers that if they produce a policy brief, then it will get noticed by relevant people and lead to policy change. The reality, of course, is that you need a clear strategy to ensure the relevant people get your brief. Simply putting it on your website is not enough. If you want an online-first strategy, this will need to be proactive, typically using social media (see Chapter 11). In addition to this, you might want to consider:

- Organising a policy webinar or seminar to 'launch' your policy brief. Consider if you want to use your policy brief as part of the marketing for your event or if you want to encourage people to attend by telling them that they will only receive the policy brief when they register for the event (of course, you can make it more widely available after the event, so this shouldn't limit the coverage of your policy brief). Consider if you have a strong enough combination of research findings and policy options to justify an event by yourself or if you might want to team up with one or two other researchers to create a combined event. By tapping into their networks and broadening the relevance to their areas of research and policy, you might get a stronger audience. When planning your webinar or seminar, consider the balance between presentations and discussion and consider integrating small-group discussions and other participatory exercises to get your audience more actively engaged with your ideas.
- Holding one-to-one meetings or small-group meetings with key individuals and teams, including those working directly in policy and those working indirectly to support or inform policy teams. Go back

to your 3i analysis to identify those you want to prioritise, sending the policy brief with an email that is tailored to their interests and needs, and you will be surprised at the number of people who agree to meet you. You can expect people to have read your policy brief ahead of your meeting, but you may still need to provide a summary. Now, rather than relying on PowerPoint, you can use your policy brief as your visual aid, keeping the meeting as informal and two-way as possible and allowing most of your time for discussion.

Finally, it is worth considering how you might repurpose your policy brief for use in other contexts. For example, you might pull out your key points and submit them to a relevant policy consultation, or you might use a former consultation response as the starting point for your conversations with members of your policy network about the focus of a future policy brief. You might want to turn your policy brief into an infographic (see Chapter 11) or extend it into a blog with links to the key pieces of evidence for those who want to dig deeper. You might want to promote your policy brief and the accompanying blog via social media to get comments on the blog and facilitate discussion on each of the social media platforms you use. And you might want to turn your key points into a presentation, for use in a webinar or seminar. Chapter 11 will review some of these other forms of communication.

Policy infographics and presentations

There are a range of other communication tools, in addition to policy briefs, that can be useful for communicating policy messages effectively. You may also want to write opinion pieces and engage with the media to influence policy informally, and you may have opportunities to give oral evidence or testimony to inquiries and committees. In this chapter, I will focus on three tools that can integrate effectively with your use of policy briefs: infographics, presentations and social media. Each has a specific use in the policy domain and can generate significant impact when used effectively. I will conclude with guidance on influencing policy through media engagement and guidance for preparing and delivering testimony to inquiries and committees.

POLICY INFOGRAPHICS AND DATA VISUALISATIONS

A policy infographic is a visual representation of evidence and policy ideas that is designed to convey information quickly and effectively to those who engage with it. They often include visualisations of data, making it easier for policy colleagues to understand complex patterns, relationships and trends or quickly grasp new insights. Depending on the communication platform, it is possible to animate and make these visualisations interactive, for example via clickable maps or decision trees that deliver relevant information based on the interests or context of the user.

Infographics and visualisations may be used in isolation, for example in the context of a microblogging platform, but even on social media they are typically used to get the attention of readers who are then directed to more detailed information. They can be easily integrated into policy briefs, presentations, websites and blogs and may be animated to include in videos.

DOI: 10.4324/9781003494942-14

If you use PowerPoint to create your infographic animation, this can then double up as a visual aid in presentations and be recorded for use in videos.

However, infographics and visualisation tools are rarely used by researchers, partly because they are perceived to be costly and time-consuming to create. In reality, there are now a number of online platforms that make it cost-effective and easy to create infographics without any design expertise. The platforms change over time, but an internet search will bring up a range of options.

While infographic platforms make it easy to create an infographic, when creating a policy infographic, you need to go through a number of initial steps to ensure that you are representing the evidence and policy options effectively:

1. First, go through the steps in the previous section to identify a relevant and timely policy challenge or evidence gap, discuss this with colleagues from your policy network and draft some text that summarises the policy challenge, the evidence and the policy options (this may become the basis for a policy brief or presentation later on).
2. Next, identify the most important challenges, pieces of evidence and options and summarise these in as few words as possible.
3. Go back over these words, shortening and simplifying as much as possible, for example using the Up-Goer Six text editor to identify jargon or an artificial intelligence text generator to suggest plain English alternatives.
4. Visualise each of these key points, drawing by hand different ideas as they come to you and discussing them with a colleague to identify alternative better ways of visually communicating each point. Your pictures don't have to look nice – the infographic platform will take care of the design later in the process.
5. Come up with a layout so that the reader is clearly directed through your points in the correct order. Bear in mind that you might want to have different layouts for use in different contexts, for example landscape for a presentation, portrait for a policy brief, or long and thin for viewing on social media on a mobile.
6. Use an online platform to convert your ideas into graphics, retaining a limited palette.
7. Integrate into social media messaging or other forms of communication as needed.

It is important to think critically about your visual choices, in case you create biases in interpretation or inadvertently play into negative stereotypes or prejudices. For example, I have seen many materials from conservationists whose key policy recommendations are around working with the people who depend upon and manage nature, but the only images are of animals and nature, or of people in traditional dress, reinforcing racial stereotypes, romanticising traditional ways of life and reinforcing the idea that humans and nature are separate. Although typically simplified in infographics, you can fall into the same traps if your representations of midwives are all female and farmers are all male or all the representations appear white (even if you colour them yellow in a well-meaning attempt to side-step this issue, given critiques of racial stereotyping in The Simpsons). Equally problematic however are choices around the scales used in graphs, maps and other visualisations. For example, changing from a linear to a logarithmic scale in a graph can radically change the shape of a relationship between variables, implying different meanings. Figure 11.1 shows an example of how abortion data was manipulated by pro-life group, Americans United for Life, by entirely removing the relevant scales. Similarly, changing the colours and thresholds for visualising map layers can be used to highlight different points, which might be used to tell quite different stories. For example, at the height of Australia's 2020 bushfires, celebrity Rihanna posted an image of the country to her 96 million followers, which looked like a satellite image, showing fires burning across the country. However, the image was in fact constructed from hotspot data from 31 days of fires, incorporating a glow effect which further exaggerated the extent of the fires. Finally, it is worth considering what evidence might be privileged or excluded by your use of infographics. For example, it is often easier to visualise quantitative data and harder to visualise the lived experiences of those affected by policy decisions.

Figures 11.2 and 11.3 show examples of policy infographics that I helped to develop. In the first infographic (Figure 11.2), the challenge is presented clearly at the top using statistics to show the scale of the problem. This then leads the eye to a series of options for avoiding the problem, with two graphics in the top left and top right of the orange box describing the two main solutions, which are then translated into actionable policy options in the bottom part of the box. Figure 11.3 was designed for integration with a policy brief, where more detailed policy suggestions

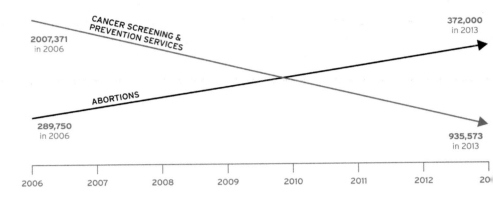

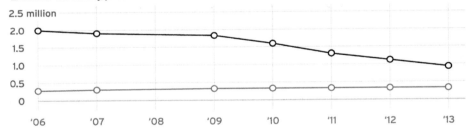

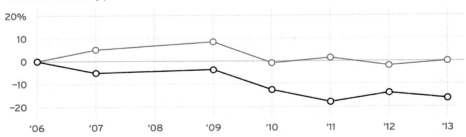

Figure 11.1 The absence of a y-axis in the top image hides how small and variable the changes in abortion procedures are, compared to the absolute (middle) and relative (bottom) decline in cancer screening procedures (credits: Americans United for Life [top] and PolitiFact [middle and bottom]).

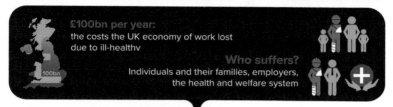

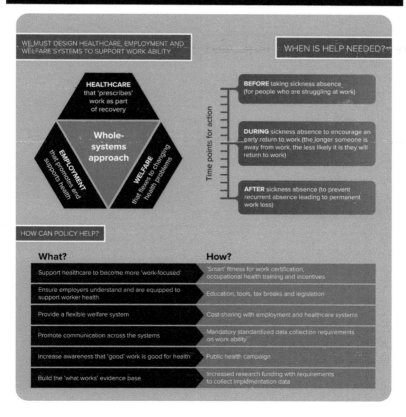

Figure 11.2 Policy infographic targeting English policies to get people who have experienced illness back to work (credit: Dr Serena Bartys and Prof Kim Burton, University of Huddersfield and Fast Track Impact).

Myths about Alcohol Intoxicated Rape Complainant's
Ability to Remember

Myth	Evidence
Testimony is more likely to be inconsistent if the complainant was alcohol-intoxicated during the rape. 	**Research to date has found no effect** of alcohol on the consistency of testimony about rape scenarios.
Complainants who were alcohol-intoxicated during the assault **will not be able to accurately remember what happened.** 	Research has found that **testimony** given by individuals who were intoxicated versus sober during rape scenarios is **less complete**, but the **accuracy of the testimony is similar.** 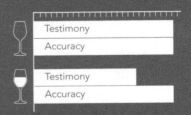
Complainants who are alcohol-intoxicated are **likely to make mistaken identifications** from lineups. 	**Research has found no effect of alcohol** on the rate of mistaken identifications in rape scenarios.

Figure 11.3 An infographic that was integrated into a policy brief targeting UK policing policies around collecting evidence from rape complainants who were intoxicated at the time of their attack (credit: Dr Heather Flowe and Fast Track Impact).

were made. The infographic focuses on the problems (framed as myths) and how the research tackles these problems (the evidence column).

An infographic, which became known as the Doughnut Model, developed by Dr Kate Raworth (Figure 11.4), has led to interest from United Nations (UN) agencies and governments seeking to move beyond growth-based economic metrics and influenced urban development policies in cities like Amsterdam, Portland and Philadelphia. Dan O'Neill from University of Leeds built on the doughnut framework to create an interactive dashboard that could be used by policy officials to design policies that encourage people to consume less, balancing quality of life with the limits of the planet, which informed Europe's 8th Environment Action Programme.

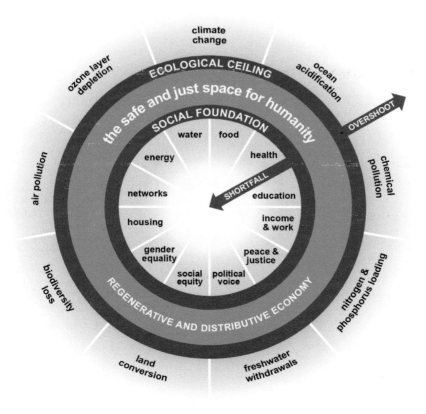

Figure 11.4 Kate Raworth's doughnut economics model (reproduced under a Creative Commons Attribution-Share Alike 4.0 International license).

Chris Cvitanovic from University of New South Wales Sydney regularly turns papers he authors into infographics, working with researcher and scientific graphic designer Stacey McCormack from Visual Knowledge Pty Ltd. Figure 11.5 provides two examples of their work: one targeted at policy bodies and organisations managing the marine environment

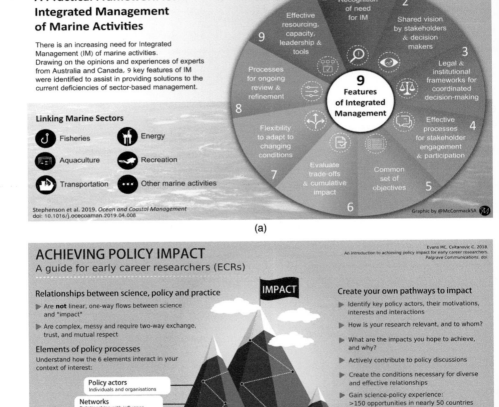

Figure 11.5 A collaboration between a researcher and graphic designer to turn papers into infographics showing one targeted at policy bodies and organisations managing the marine environment (a) and one summarising guidance to early career researchers seeking policy impact (b) (credit: Stacey McCormack, Visual Knowledge Pty Ltd).

and one summarising messages from paper with Megan Evans providing guidance to early career researchers seeking policy impact.

Data visualisations can be as simple as Figure 5.1 in Chapter 5 where I summarised the complex landscape of organisations relevant to ecosystem markets in the UK, arranged in groups and sub-groups using coloured circles in PowerPoint. In Figure 11.6, my colleagues and I sought to communicate the outcomes of a process we codesigned with the UN Environment Programme (you can see our Theory of Change in Figure 8.1 in Chapter 8) to standardise the data governments and researchers collect about peatlands, to facilitate evidence synthesis that could inform future policies. The paper was full to the brim with long tables until we started thinking about how we would communicate our findings to policy colleagues, which led us to the visualisations in Figure 11.6, which attempt to show at a glance all the variables that should be considered, which were agreed to be the most important (having met a threshold of 70%

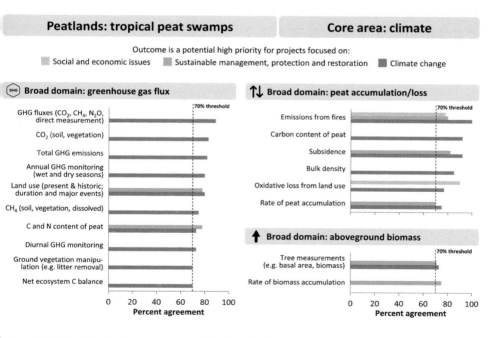

Figure 11.6 Visualisation showing the variables that should be measured by governments and researchers assessing the role of peatlands in climate change, showing which variables were agreed to be important by >70% of experts who were consulted and which of these are most relevant to measure if the project or policy is seeking climate, socio-economic or sustainability outcomes (reproduced under a CC-BY licence).

expert agreement) for any of three policy goals. I'll let you decide if you think we succeeded in communicating that data effectively or not, but you can see how data visualisation can enhance your research as well as your impact (we dumped the tables and went visual for our paper as well as our policy engagement).

POLICY SLIDE DECKS AND PRESENTATIONS AT POLICY EVENTS

A policy presentation is a talk by a researcher (possibly accompanied by other researchers or non-academic speakers as co-presenters) outlining evidence for policy options for discussion with an audience. It may or may not be accompanied by visual aids.

When accompanied by well-designed slides, the slides themselves may become a useful means of communication with wider policy audiences. My former colleague Niki Rust, who now advises UK governments via the Committee on Climate Change and used to work in a government department and at Worldwide Fund for Nature, recently posted on social media platform X, 'I am constantly amazed at how prevalent the slidedeck is for influencing policy. Think: PowerPoint or it didn't happen. Think how best to convey your messages to time-poor people'.

There are a number of contexts in which you give presentations to a policy audience, and your approach will need to be tailored to these circumstances. For example, you may have:

- Been called to provide oral evidence to an inquiry or hearing. In this case you might not be allowed to bring visual aids, but there is nothing to stop you handing out a supporting policy brief with your main points. The structure and clarity of your talk will be even more important if you don't have slides to help signpost your points visually.
- Been invited to present your work to a policy audience in a seminar, webinar or meeting, for example as part of a technical committee, an end-of-project meeting and a policy conference or as part of a regular seminar series.
- Created your own policy event where, instead of you being invited, you are inviting policy colleagues to attend your seminar, webinar or conference.

You do not have a guaranteed audience in any of these settings (attendance may be poor even at events organised by policy organisations), but if you are doing the inviting, you will need to work especially hard at targeting a highly relevant and important issue and marketing your event effectively. Although social media can be a useful way to get interest across policy networks, consider asking policy colleagues to promote it via internal email lists and intranet message boards to which you do not have access and consider writing personal invitations to members of key teams, with the option to follow up via a one-to-one meeting for these key individuals if they can't make the time and date you have selected. Consider the time of day and week when you hold your event, the location (in close proximity to a key department you want to target, for example) and whether you can afford to turn it into a drinks reception or lunchtime event, to incentivise more people to attend.

The most important thing you need to get right is the content, so follow the instructions for generating targeted, evidence-based messages that I proposed for writing policy briefs earlier in this chapter, to make sure that you are able to defend every point you make. A talk might feel more informal, especially if you tend to ad lib, but you could be filmed or live quoted on social media and create confusion and worse if you say things in an oral presentation that you would not be prepared to put down on paper. For particularly risky topics and in high-stakes situations, it may be safer to read from a script that you have rehearsed and part-memorised so that it still looks natural, to avoid inadvertently 'mis-speaking' (as politicians are fond of calling it).

Once you have your content, your next challenge is to adapt this to your audience and context. For example, your time limit will have a strong influence on what you are able to say and how much audience engagement you have time to elicit. The seniority of your audience matters. For more junior audiences of analysts, you might want to include more research and detail, and for more senior audiences of decision-makers, you might want to focus more on the policy options in a simpler and shorter format. The diversity of your audience also matters. Although you might have targeted your event to a specific policy community, you may have attendees from academia, the third-sector and practice-based agencies and other organisations responsible for policy delivery. You will need to decide if you want to tailor your talk to all of the different audiences in attendance or just focus on a subset, for example not providing the methodological detail you know the academic attendees would like.

Then, for each of the key audiences who have quite different needs and interests, you will need to think about how to ensure your points resonate effectively with each group. This may require you to explain, frame or contextualise points in multiple ways, which could slow you down. Finally, you will need to adapt to the physical setting in which you are working. If you are talking in a noisy atrium, then you might want to organise a microphone or arrange seats in a close circle where everyone will be able to hear. If you want to facilitate audience engagement via a sticky note exercise, you will need to make sure you have permission to stick flip chart paper on the walls. It is not always possible to predict who will turn up to your presentation, so it is worth turning up early to look at attendance lists or to speak informally to guests before the event starts to get a sense of the likely diversity of your audience so that you can adapt on the day.

There are a number of ways you can structure your content, and you might want to retain the same order I proposed for the content of a policy brief in Chapter 10. One particularly effective structure that can keep your audience spellbound hinges on your ability to create narrative tension as you deliver your talk:

1. Build curiosity or intrigue. Explain the policy challenge or problem you will be addressing and why it is important. Explain what is currently unknown, to build a sense of intrigue, and explain why the existing or obvious answers are unlikely to work, deepening the curiosity of your audience.
2. Reveal the answer. Explain the evidence, starting slowly from the level of your audience, using examples and metaphors to build concepts up progressively until your audience understands the policy options you are proposing and their evidence base.
3. Explain the relevance or make a call to action. A more passive option for concluding your talk is to return to the original challenge and explain exactly why your suggestions are so relevant and important, allowing your audience to decide what they should do next. Alternatively, you

might take the more active option of creating a call to action. This doesn't have to be the creation of a new policy or regulation. It could be a call for a pilot or trial, or for a working group to discuss the viability of a pilot scheme.

Other possible structures include demonstrations and case studies where policy outcomes in a test case or comparable country act as the evidence base for a discussion on the relevance of the ideas in the context of your policy audience. Alternatively, rather than relying on the suspense of the three-step structure above, you might reveal the end of the journey before explaining how you got there and how others can follow this example to solve similar problems in their own context.

If you are using slides, their design can either help or hinder your influence. Stay away from complex graphs and tables and text-heavy slides that you are effectively using as your notes; consider instead an animated infographic visual style (see the previous section: Policy infographics and data visualisations) or a more photographic style, using images as visual metaphors to emphasise key points, with keywords only on the slides. In both cases, you will need a strategy for keeping your notes in front of you, bearing in mind that there might not be a lectern for you to place your notes on. Whether or not you are allowed to bring a PowerPoint presentation, you might want to consider bringing a policy brief. Not only will this serve as an additional visual aid and provide people with a way to get in touch with you after your talk but it will also allow you to have details at your fingertips and summarise key points in less time, making more time for discussion.

There are many resources available on voice coaching and presentation style (see Further Reading, in particular the chapter on presenting with impact in *The Research Impact Handbook*), so I will restrict ourselves to a few key points on this. Give particular thought to the first minute of your talk, considering how you will get your audience's attention and establish your credibility. It is important to know your audience well enough to be able to frame the benefits of listening to your talk in tangible terms that you know will motivate your audience. However, no matter how motivated they are to get these benefits, your audience will switch off and down-weight what you say, if they do not believe you have the credibility or authority to deliver your message. If you are an early career researcher, consider headlining the brands of your funders and university or bringing copies of peer-reviewed papers you have written that you've drawn on in your talk. If you don't have your doctorate yet, refer to yourself as a postgraduate researcher rather than a PhD student.

If you are lacking in confidence, seek out training and opportunities to practise and identify the habits that most strongly communicate your nerves, working to overcome them. For example, if you get the shakes, make sure you use a lectern for your notes to avoid the pieces of paper amplifying the shakes. If you sway, pace or twist yourself into knots as you speak, practise standing with your feet planted firmly on the ground. If you don't know what to do with your hands, practise confident hand gestures or decide to hold them comfortably in front of you. If you use verbal fillers, like 'erm' and 'um', work hard on replacing these with short pauses, recording yourself and watching back until you get them under control. This is important because we are taught from an early age we can detect a liar by looking for a disconnect between what a person says and the way they say it – their body language will give them away. We also have a tendency to mirror those we are interacting with emotionally. As a result, we instinctively start to feel nervous when we are listening to a nervous speaker, which can be distracting, and we instinctively start to doubt the validity of an evidence-based message spoken nervously. In contrast, we may have to work extra hard to listen critically to a lobbyist delivering a message that runs contrary to the evidence with particular confidence and flair.

Finally, consider the extent to which you want to engage with your audience. At minimum, you need to make sure you make ample time for discussion. If the organiser has told you to speak for 20 minutes and leave 10 minutes for discussion, consider explaining that you will only talk for 15 minutes so that you can split the time equally between your presentation and the discussion. If that's not enough time for you to get through all your points, then bring along a policy brief or print out copies of your paper and leave them at the back of the room and refer people to those for the details so that you can make time for more discussion. However, you might want to do something more participatory, for example asking people to discuss a question with their neighbour for two to three minutes or splitting into small group if you have longer and think this would engage a higher proportion of your audience than plenary discussion. You might use a technique like a 'metaplan', using sticky notes in person or Google Jamboard (or similar) online to get everyone in the room to provide a fixed number of ideas per person (one per sticky note) in answer to an open question. Working with your audience, you can cluster these and use them to focus small-group discussion or thematically order questions in a plenary discussion.

At the end of your presentation, you might want to use the 'postcard to your future self' approach to find out who attended and get permission to follow them up later. Place postcards on everyone's seat with an image linked to the session on the front, and a General Data Protection Regulation (GDPR)-compliant tick box on the back, inviting participants at the end to tell you one thing they want to do in policy or practice based on what they learned during the session. Then, post these back to everyone after a month so they get a reminder from themselves to do the action they wrote down, and for those who ticked the box, you can follow up to find out how they are getting on, offering help if necessary. You can also then contact them a few months later with a survey to find out more about how the impact of your workshop might be developing. You can do this online by inviting participants to write the answer to this question in the chat, providing their email if they want to give you permission to follow up. For more ideas, have a look at the chapters on facilitating and designing workshops in *The Research Impact Handbook* and the blog on 'Tips and tools for making your online meetings and workshops more interactive' that I wrote with Sawsan Khuri in Further Reading.

In addition to helping you create more powerful slide decks and presentations, infographics and visualisations can help you create more effective policy briefs that clearly communicate complex research quickly and effectively. However, it is important to take a critical approach to the use of visual tools in policy work, given the potential for misunderstanding and bias. Just having nice slides is not enough to maintain interest and get your audience to engage deeply with your work. I wish I had known the presentation tips I have shared with you in this chapter earlier in my career because I used to treat policy slide decks and presentations the same way I treated conference presentations to other researchers. It turns out that your research colleagues will also thank you, if you apply some of these tips to your next conference talk. By creating a simple, memorable message and delivering it confidently and empathically, it is possible to connect with your audience and get them to think deeply about the ideas you have to share with the world. But infographics and presentations are just two of a number of ways of communicating with policy colleagues, and in Chapter 12, I want to cover some of the other common approaches you may want to take.

Other ways to influence policy

There are more ways of working with policy than it is possible to cover in any depth in a book of this length, but there are still a number of other important ways you might want to engage, which deserve some attention. In this chapter, I will consider some of the opportunities and challenges associated with more indirect approaches to influencing policy using social and mass media. I will then briefly consider how you might testify to legislative bodies via inquiries and committees; respond to policy consultations; apply for policy fellowships, shadowing schemes and internships; and engage in commissioned research for policy bodies.

INFLUENCING POLICY VIA SOCIAL AND MASS MEDIA

Although an indirect means of influencing policy, engaging with social and mass media can be important ways of mobilising public opinion and building your credibility and profile as a researcher, engendering trust with policy colleagues. However, given the indirect route to policy, these methods are often not a very efficient use of your time. I know of many researchers who can provide long lists of media mentions, show me interviews and who have impressive social media statistics, who cannot actually tell me what real-world benefit has arisen from all this work. It is possible to build trusting relationships with policy colleagues without having a media profile, and working with individuals and small groups informally is a lower risk approach, given the potential for journalists to twist words and conduct aggressive interviews.

Nevertheless, where you have a degree of editorial control, engaging with the media via articles in *The Conversation* or writing opinion articles

DOI: 10.4324/9781003494942-15

and editorials is relatively low risk and can be a useful way of getting your research to a wide audience. Although this is a bit of a scatter gun approach, if you do not already have strong policy networks and credible pathways to policy impact, engaging with mass media can be a useful way to make connections with non-academic organisations working on the same issues. For example, my peatland impacts started when *The Guardian* newspaper picked up on part of a paper I co-authored during my PhD, suggesting that carbon markets might in future be able to pay for peatland restoration. This led to a call from a charity restoring peat bogs who wanted to know how they could access funding from carbon markets. I had no idea but told them that if they would be willing to collaborate on some funding bids, then we could try and work it out together.

There are many others better placed than I am to advise you on how best to get and then manage media attention for your work. However, little of the literature and training available focuses on impact, with success measured in reach rather than the actual benefits achieved. For this reason, I have found guidance from the campaigning literature particularly useful, for example Chris Rose's 2010 book, *How to Win Campaigns: Communications for Change*.

Social media can also be used to influence policy both directly and indirectly. Indirectly, social media campaigns have been used to influence public discourse and change public attitudes, which can in turn lead to pressure on governments to change policy. However, researchers are more likely to influence policy directly through engagement with politicians (some of whom are more accessible than ever before via social media) and civil servants, promoting evidence and policy messages in a more targeted way than might otherwise be possible. In the UK, it is possible to follow and interact with some politicians and government ministers on X, and LinkedIn's search function enables you to identify civil servants by the government department or agency they work in, alongside keywords linked to policy and research areas. Some politicians and civil servants regularly crowdsource ideas via social media and may be receptive to ideas they receive from researchers in response to these requests.

Others follow researchers and engage with their content more passively. If your research and expertise is highly visible on social media, you increase the likelihood that members of policy networks preferentially find and use your work. Having a Google Scholar profile is helpful, and it is important to ensure as many of your papers as possible are open access. But there is a difference between research that is accessible and research that is understandable, and social media is a powerful way of helping people understand your work, whether through the use of blogs and vlogs to unpack and explain research in plain language or by engaging in conversation with readers through microblogging platforms to answer questions and explain your work.

By engaging with relevant policy networks on social media, it is possible for researchers to become aware of policy challenges and opportunities that they might otherwise miss, and if they are highly visible and accessible via these platforms, they may get asked to help others seeking to influence policy on the topics they are researching. Many researchers talk about serendipitous impacts, when unplanned impacts arise from their work. However, the majority of these impacts have one thing in common: the researcher just happened to be in the right place at the right time. Social media makes it easier than ever for you to be that researcher, embedded in the right networks, accessible and approachable, so that when opportunities arise, people think of you and your research.

If you want to achieve a specific policy impact, though, you will need to be more proactive, and developing a social media strategy can help you use your time online efficiently. To do this, you don't need to create a document; you just need to be able to answer these four questions:

1. What policy impacts do you want to achieve via social media?
2. Who are you trying to reach, what are they interested in and what platforms are they on?
3. How can you make your content actionable, shareable and rewarding for those who interact with you so that you can start building relationships and move the conversation from social media to real life?
4. Who can you work with to make your use of social media more efficient and effective?

For more information about creating a social media strategy for impact, you can download a social media strategy template and Logic Model at www.fasttrackimpact.com/i-want-more-impact-online.

However, engaging with social media is fraught with challenges, especially when debates become heated or offensive and when attempts to use evidence for societal benefits attract negative attention from groups whose interests might be compromised by your work. For those who do not wish to take too many risks on social media, it is possible to discover many policy opportunities with a private account from which you only read, without ever having to generate any of your own content or engage in conversations. You may also work with institutional accounts and others in your network who have relevant social media followings to get content to relevant groups, without having to have an account yourself. Many books have been written on this subject, so I will not discuss social media in depth here (see in particular Mark Carrigan's *Social Media for Academics* and the relevant chapters in the *Research Impact Handbook* – see Further Reading). However, it is worth noting that each of the forms of communication in this chapter and the previous chapter can be repurposed for social media (including presentations via SlideShare or video recordings).

I have personally used policy briefs, infographics, policy presentations and social media to generate impacts from my research on peatlands. The first policy brief that the team produced was developed without any input from policy colleagues; it was thematic and contained no actionable policy options, and it had no impact. Five more policy briefs were produced over the course of the research, each engaging policy colleagues more strongly in their production and targeting specific and pertinent issues. The team visited Defra and presented their research in invited policy seminars and one-to-one meetings with key individuals and teams. These activities built sufficient interest that Defra then funded additional research to explore the development of a policy mechanism. The Peatland Code was launched in 2015, ten years after the research started. The team then launched a public awareness campaign in collaboration with two charities that were active in the policy space using infographics and a music video (Figure 12.1) to communicate the urgency of restoring damaged peatlands. This reached members of the international policy community who used the Peatland Code as a basis for creating international resolutions, which in turn influenced national peatland policies around the world.

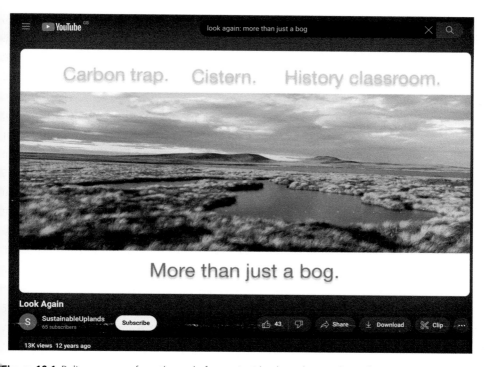

Figure 12.1 Policy message from the end of a music video based on evidence from peatland research.

TESTIFYING TO INQUIRIES AND COMMITTEES

As a researcher, you may be invited to give evidence to a legislative body, for example to senate and parliament, or to an inquiry or committee, helping directly inform policy decisions. You may be invited because of your profile on a particular topic, or if you are less well-known, you may be invited on the basis of written evidence you have submitted to the process. You may be invited alone or as part of a panel of expert witnesses. You may or may not be allowed to use visual aids, but in cases where I have been told not to use slides, nobody has stopped me from handing round copies of a policy brief.

Good preparation is essential, and by following my advice in the previous chapter on co-producing and stress-testing policy briefs, you should be able to build a robust evidence base for a small number of key messages or policy options, tailored to the needs of your audience. The guidance above on creating slide decks and presenting to policy audiences gives you a number of options for structuring your material for oral delivery. If you are able to use visuals to add further impact to your testimony, the advice I've given earlier in this chapter should enable you to keep your message clear and memorable.

It is also worth preparing for the kinds of questions you are likely to receive. In some cases, you will be given these in advance, and you might therefore want to structure your talk around these questions. In other cases, you will need to brainstorm likely questions with colleagues in your policy networks, to try and predict and prepare for the most likely questions. It is important to keep your answers as succinct as possible so that there is time for everyone who wants to ask you questions to do so. You may get asked questions you cannot answer, or do not feel comfortable answering, and in this case you can say that you will get them a written answer later or refuse to answer. I once watched an excruciating Select Committee in UK Parliament on the impacts of Brexit, with a panel of four academics. A pro-Brexit politician started the session by asking each academic how they had voted in the referendum. Like the majority of other academics in the country, each in turn disclosed that they had vote to remain in Europe. The politician proceeded to use this answer to invalidate any evidence they might then present suggesting that Brexit would lead to negative impacts, saying words to the effect of, 'you would say that, wouldn't you?'. Of course, none of the academics were under any obligation to answer such a personal question. But once the first academic had answered the question, it would have taken a lot of courage to be the only one who refused to give an answer.

RESPONDING TO POLICY CONSULTATIONS

There are often more opportunities to respond to consultations and provide evidence to inquiries and committees than you have time. In the UK, where many policy areas are devolved to the four countries of England, Scotland, Wales and Northern Ireland, deadlines for these opportunities are often close together, and it is not realistic to try and prioritise each one. I therefore try and assess the likely impact arising from a consultation, prioritising consultations on significant changes in legislation over more minor changes to regulations or the development of new strategies, guidelines and the like. Even then, I don't have time to respond to all the consultations I would like to. I therefore try and respond as a team wherever possible, inputting to consultations being led by organisations in my policy networks or coordinating researchers in my institution or project teams to share the burden of responding to the numerous questions contained in most exercises of this sort. In many cases, we will only respond to a small proportion of the questions asked, to which we have answers based on evidence from our work. If you ask for inputs from colleagues via email, there is a danger that you will get too much material, and much may not be relevant or easy to understand. This leads to a lot of editing work and disappointed colleagues who can't find their contributions in the work you submit. I therefore prefer to do this in workshop mode, writing each of the questions on pieces of flip chart paper around the room and inviting answers on initialled sticky notes. I can then summarise the most relevant ideas, following up with specific questions via email later, to expand on the material I think will be most useful.

Many consultations and calls for written evidence will have word or page limits that will prevent you from writing too extensively, but where this is not the case, it is important that you provide concise answers, in accessible language, and provide references to the research that underpins your answers. I often find that this process helps me and my teams understand the current focus of our policy colleagues, and I will often turn our consultation response into a policy brief. This then enables me to follow up individually with key members of relevant teams to share more detailed answers and answer follow-up questions. Whether or not this leads to an invitation to present the findings more formally, for example to a committee, it is good to know that at least one relevant person has engaged with and understood your evidence.

POLICY FELLOWSHIPS, SHADOWING AND INTERNSHIPS

In addition to the more informal relationships I have suggested you might build in earlier chapters, you might want to consider applying for a policy fellowship, internship or shadowing scheme. The availability of such schemes differs between countries and fields of research, with many opportunities focussing on more applied fields. They also vary in the extent to which they cover your costs, from travel expenses only to covering your salary. Most of these opportunities are focussed around evidence to support the development of a specific policy or a policy-relevant output, such as an evidence synthesis, background briefing paper or set of policy options. In other cases, you may be inducted into a policy or evidence team, working with colleagues to respond to the urgent demands of the day.

Whatever your role is like, it will provide you with a unique insight into the mechanics of government and the challenges and constraints faced by your policy colleagues, enabling you to build more empathic relationships with others in similar roles in future. You are also likely to bring back numerous insights to your academic role, both from the breadth of evidence you will have engaged with and from the colleagues you have been able to work with, who have often worked across multiple departments on many wider issues, giving them unique perspectives you can learn from.

The trust that you are able to gain through positions like these often means that the same policy team will follow up regularly with you in future to ask questions, giving you ongoing access to their work. I applied for multiple pieces of commissioned research from the government department in which I did my first fellowship and was rejected in every case. After the fellowship, my policy colleagues regularly sent me the tenders, suggesting that I applied, and a few years later, for a brief spell, my entire salary was covered in contracts with the department. Serena Bartys from University of Huddersfield also used policy fellowship to generate impact from her work enabling people with long-term health conditions to continue working (Box 12.1). Unlike me

---

Box 12.1 Combining commissioned research, infographics, policy briefs and a policy fellowship to influence health policy.

Work disability due to ill-health is a leading global concern, costing the UK economy alone around £100 billion per year. It is a major cause of disadvantage and inequality, placing a considerable burden on health, employment and welfare systems.

Serena Bartys from University of Huddersfield conducted commissioned research for England's Department for Work and Pensions, the Health and Safety Executive, the Association for British Insurers and Public Health England to show that, through an early, biopsychosocial approach with integrated health and employment systems, work disability is largely avoidable.

She used a policy fellowship in England's Joint Work and Health Unit to inform the development of a Green Paper, Improving Lives: Work, Health and Disability in 2016. This, combined with a policy brief featuring the infographic in Figure 11.2, led to a shift in understanding, by policymakers and key healthcare and employment organisations, of how work can be health-supportive. This reconceptualisation is now reflected in national and international policy and guidance relevant to all working-age people.

rather than unlocking contract work, her policy fellowship built on many years of previous contract work for various government departments, in which she had co-produced the evidence for the policy impact with policy colleagues.

POLICY SPRINTS

Most engagement with policy is fairly slow and methodical, often moving at the pace of the research process, which tends to be measured in years. However, most policy problems require urgent attention, with answers expected in days, weeks or months. This is where policy sprints can provide policy ideas that are both rapid and rigorous. Policy sprints are a focused, time-bound and collaborative method of developing options that are responsive to immediate needs and emerging issues. They borrow from the principles of design thinking, agile project management and rapid prototyping to create an adaptive and flexible environment in which to explore policy challenges with a range of relevant groups. This may include different policy teams and agency staff alongside researchers from different disciplines and groups affected by the issue. The process encourages regular iteration and refinement of ideas, subjecting policy options to testing, feedback and improvement to make sure that they will work in a range of changing contexts. As such, the process typically proceeds through the following stages:

- **Problem Framing**: The sprint begins with a clear identification of the problem or challenge at hand, based on existing research and interviews and workshops with those affected by the issue, to gain a deep understanding of the problem.
- **Ideation**: Once the problem is defined, teams brainstorm potential solutions. Creativity is encouraged, and no idea is dismissed outright, as the goal is to generate a wide range of possible policy options.
- **Prototyping**: Teams select one or more promising policy ideas and create detailed prototypes, in the form of policy documents, drafts of legislation or even pilot programs.
- **Testing and Feedback**: Prototypes are tested in real-world pilots or through computer simulations, alongside feedback from experts and other relevant parties to refine the policy ideas.

- **Implementation and Evaluation**: After sufficient testing and feedback, the policy is refined and prepared for implementation (depending on the nature of the policy, this may involve parliamentary scrutiny). Monitoring and evaluation mechanisms are put in place to assess the policy's impact and effectiveness.
- **Continuous Improvement**: Even after implementation, policy sprints remain active. Evaluation ensures that policies remain responsive to changing conditions and emerging challenges.

I have heard these processes used more informally over longer periods of time as 'open policy-making', where the idea is to open the policy-making process to groups outside the traditional policy-making community, evaluating policy ideas on their merits, regardless of their source. But I like the clear purpose, structure and iteration of policy sprints as an approach, in comparison to the more informal processes I've been part of in the past. Policy sprints will not be suitable for all policy issues, but they offer a valuable tool for addressing urgent problems in a constantly changing world.

COMMISSIONED RESEARCH

Research can be commissioned by public bodies, ranging from government bodies to delivery agencies, to support policy development, implementation or evaluation. I have been actively persuaded against applying for this sort of work by numerous Universities, and in one institution I had to make a case for doing this work to my Head of School before being allowed to apply. There are a number of reasons for this. First, many policy organisations do not pay the significant overhead charges made by Universities, effectively requiring Heads of School to subsidise the research from other sources, to pay the University for the services used in the School. Second, commissioned work for policy bodies is by definition national in scope and so is unlikely to form the basis of an academic contribution of international significance. Moreover, such work does not require the same levels of rigour as academic research, which would take too long and cost too much, further limiting the potential for academic publications from these projects. Finally, policy colleagues can be demanding clients, often requiring significant revisions of policy reports written by academics who do not understand the brief, given how different the requirements are, compared to academic funders. As a result, projects can take significantly more time than anticipated, impacting on other duties. One way to get around this is to work through your policy networks to identify consultancies applying for the contract, offering a small number of days at the University's consultancy rate so that you aren't losing money and you have an opportunity for impact, without the time commitment of leading the project yourself.

One of the reasons I struggled to win these sorts of contracts as a researcher who was not known to the government department I was targeting is that academics have a bad reputation for doing these sorts of contracts badly. To this day, I still regularly get negative feedback from policy colleagues telling me to put all the detail in appendices and asking me to rewrite the report in a fraction of the number of pages I gave them in my first draft. But I comfort myself in the knowledge that most of my colleagues have seen much worse. One such colleague told me about her worst experience working with an academic who asked for an extension, which she denied because she needed his evidence for a policy deadline that she couldn't shift. He proceeded to grant himself the deadline he had requested and missed her deadline, so the research was worthless to her when she eventually received it. Nevertheless, she put it out to review and received three very negative reports from other academics who questioned the methods and findings of his research. She requested revisions, and instead of making the changes suggested by his reviewers, he sent a long rebuttal, explaining why the reviewers were wrong. Then, to add insult to injury, he was talking at a policy conference in a session chaired by my policy colleague, and to her horror, he presented his unrevised results, boldly proclaiming that the research had been funded by the government. Not knowing what to do next, she sat on the report, but the researcher was unhappy that it had not been published, and so sent Freedom of Information requests to force publication of his report. Eventually, she published the report but took the unprecedented step of also publishing a disclaimer, the reviews and his dismissive responses to the reviews alongside the report. To give the researcher his due, it was a controversial issue and he believed that both the government and his reviewers had taken the wrong side of the debate and were not giving him a fair hearing.

This is a common complaint from researchers who engage with commissioned research, who are constrained in what they can write by heavy editing from policy colleagues who hold opposing views to those of the researcher. Alternatively, instead of challenging the research directly, reports may simply never be published, enabling politicians to ignore advice from the researcher without embarrassment. The only time this happened to one of my reports was when I was particularly critical of how a particular publicly funded scheme was wasting money. The scheme was quietly changed and my report was never published, avoiding embarrassment, but ultimately saving taxpayers' money, so I never pushed for the report to be published.

To avoid this sort of thing happening to you, it is essential that you clearly negotiate your terms of engagement at the outset. This is likely to include a much more detailed work plan and list of milestones and deliverables than you would include in a research project. Also look closely at your contract and request changes if you want to have the right to publish the research as an academic article after the project has finished. Make sure you talk in detail about exactly what your policy colleagues are expecting from the research so that you can manage expectations if necessary and make a plan that delivers what they need in good time.

In Chapters 12-14, I have considered some of the key practical methods you can use to engage with policy colleagues, targeting relevant teams, understanding and addressing their challenges and considering the best ways to communicate the evidence they need. However, there is still one essential step you need to take. In any conversation, you regularly check that you are following each other, and if one of you isn't keeping up, you backtrack and explain things again. If you are not evaluating your impact you will have no way of knowing if anyone is listening to you (let alone understanding what you are saying). Without evaluating your work with policy colleagues, you will not know if your work is delivering benefits or wasting your time (and theirs). This is the topic of the penultimate chapter.

CHAPTER 13

Evaluating policy impacts

Policy impacts are notoriously difficult to evaluate and evidence. There are often significant time lags between the publication of research and actual policy change, and ideological barriers can block and delay progress indefinitely in some policy areas. In addition to evidence from research, many other factors influence policy decisions. Even when research is a major driver of policy, there are usually many studies by different groups, making it difficult to attribute impacts to any given team, project or publication. However, it is crucial that we are able to understand whether or not our research and engagement are leading to policy impacts. Partly, this is because we need formative feedback to enhance our policy engagement practice. If everything we are trying isn't working, then we need to know so that we can stop wasting everyone's time and try something else. Increasingly, our funders and universities also want summative evidence that our research has led to policy impacts to showcase impacts and help justify public investment in research. So, how do you evaluate policy impacts?

IMPACT MONITORING MADE EASY

The answer is not simple, but it should always start with monitoring your impact. I will discuss the challenges and options for evaluating impact later in this chapter, but if you have been keeping track of your impacts throughout the engagement process, then your task will be much easier. However, few researchers regularly or systematically monitor their impacts. Partly this is due to a perception that monitoring impact is time-consuming and complex. To an extent this is true, if you adopt a traditional approach, but there are quick and easy solutions as well.

The classic way to monitor policy impacts is to use indicators. Indicators are typically established at the start of the engagement process, as part

DOI: 10.4324/9781003494942-16

of your impact plan, possibly as part of a Logic Model or Theory of Change (see Chapter 5). Some will be indicators of successful engagement (rather than impact), for example strong attendance at policy seminars or webinars. Others will be impact indicators, but they will be milestones you would expect to see on the pathway to policy impact rather than the ultimate impacts you are hoping to see, for example citations in minor strategic documents such as action plans and committee reports. Still others will be indicators of actual impacts, for example, changes in policy, regulation and guidelines linked to your research, or evidence that these policies are actually generating public benefits once they have been implemented (e.g. using national statistics).

In addition to identifying relevant indicators, you need to work out how you will collect the data, for example if your institution has a subscription, you can run regular checks on your key papers via services like Overton and Altmetric to see if they've been cited in policy documents (Figure 13.1). Depending on the indicators you select, you may want to collect and analyse feedback from policy seminars and webinars, collect social media statistics or keep track of national statistics. To use this data as formative feedback, you will need to review progress towards your indicators regularly, checking if you need to change the indicators you're measuring and adapting your engagement strategy if the indicators suggest you are not likely to achieve your desired impacts.

All this takes time and perseverance, however, and unless you have a particularly well-resourced project with a team member dedicated to impact, you probably don't have time to be identifying and tracking indicators on a regular basis. That's why I encourage researchers to create some sort of 'dumping ground' for anything they think might constitute evidence of impact. You need to find something quick and easy that you are likely to use on a day-to-day basis. Ideally it should be backed up and accessible to your teams, not just you. That way, anyone in your team can add evidence, and you can check in regularly with your team during meetings, getting people to add any evidence that might have emerged since the last meeting. Some people use shared Google Docs and Sheets for this purpose. Microsoft Teams channels and OneNote have a dedicated email address so that you can email evidence of impact to a dedicated impact channel. The benefit of this (compared to just keeping things in your inbox or an email folder) is that you can keep everything in one place

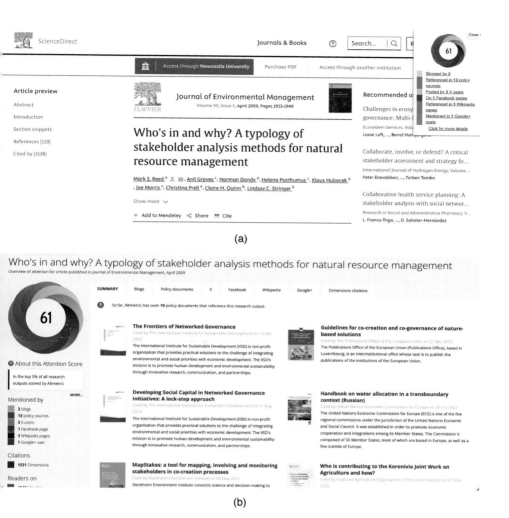

Figure 13.1 Screenshots of an article, showing its Altmetric score (a) and the policy documents citing the article (b), captured 10 January 2024.

and invite others from your team to contribute their evidence to the same channel, without having to log into a system or interrupt your workflow. You can email almost anything to yourself, from videos and voice memos to social media mentions, without leaving the app. The key thing is that you actually use your dumping ground. There is no need to think long and hard about whether or not something is impactful enough or what sort of impact it might be. Just put it there, and when you are next looking for impact, you will be able to assess what's relevant. If you don't have something like this, I encourage you to think about it now. I guarantee you that you will thank yourself the next time someone asks you what your impact is, and you're not left trawling through your memory, calendar, emails, likes and bookmarks to try and remember what happened.

EVALUATING POLICY IMPACTS

Impact evaluation is 'the process of assessing the significance and reach of both positive and negative effects of research' (see Reed et al., 2021, in Further Reading). As such, your task is deceptively simple: you need to identify cause and effect relationships between research (as the cause) and impact (as the effect). Your goal is to create an evidence-based argument that your research was sufficient (or at least necessary) to generate impacts that were significant and far-reaching.

The significance of an impact can be defined as the magnitude or intensity of the effect of research on individuals, groups or organisations. Reach can be defined as the number, extent or diversity of individuals, groups or organisations that benefit from research. Reach can be understood in two ways:

- Scaling-out refers to an impact spreading socially (from one individual, community, organisation or interest group to another) and/or spatially (e.g. from the farm to the catchment level or from one state or country to another); and
- Scaling-up and scaling-down refer to an impact reaching a higher or lower institutional or governance level, for example scaling-up from influencing individual behaviour change and changing policy mechanisms (e.g. regulation) to influencing the policy frameworks within which those mechanisms sit. Alternatively, scaling-up could range from changing individual perceptions to social learning (where ideas spread through social networks to become situated in communities of practice or social units). To take another example, scaling-up could range from informal changes in individual professional practice to changes in codes of conduct, professional guidance or organisational practice. These processes can operate in reverse, where impacts scale-down from higher to lower institutional or governance levels, for example evidence-based policies, operationalised through regulation, may lead to individual behaviour change.

These two dimensions of reach are linked in the sense that scaling-up an impact to higher institutional levels increases the probability of more widespread adoption of ideas, practices and other changes that reach new beneficiaries at wider social or spatial scales. Analysis of highly rated impact case studies from the UK's Research Excellence Framework (REF2014) (see Reichard et al., 2020, in Further Reading) shows that the most convincing impacts included specific, high-magnitude and well-evidenced articulations of significance and reach. However, they also clearly established causal links between research and impact.

The causal relationship between research and impact can be: i) necessary, implying that a body of research was necessary to generate the impact but could not alone have caused the impact (i.e. the research was a significant contributing factor among other causes but was not sufficient alone to generate the impact); or ii) sufficient, implying that a body of research alone was sufficient to generate the impact. A 'body of research' could range from a body of evidence within a single project or programme to a body of work by a single researcher or group or a wider body of research by multiple authors and teams on a given topic.

As such, the task of any impact evaluation is to establish whether or not there is a causal relationship between research and impact, providing evidence that the research was necessary (at least) or sufficient (at best). Necessary and sufficient cause can be established in a number of ways (see Reed et al., 2021, in Further Reading), ranging from triangulating multiple informal sources of evidence to more resource-intensive methods such as randomised control trials. Given the wide range of different types of impact you might be able to have in any given policy domain, it is clear that no one method or approach will enable you to evaluate every policy impact. Instead, you need to adapt your evaluation to:

- Your time and resources (in particular whether you are doing this yourself or can hire in help);
- The skills available to you (especially if you are doing the evaluation yourself) and how you view the world and what constitutes valid knowledge (your ontology and epistemology, to use the social science jargon);
- The type of impact you are evaluating (e.g. you will need very different methods to determine whether a new policy was influenced by your

research, compared to evaluating whether the policy you influenced actually delivered public benefits once it was implemented);
- Whether you are trying to establish that your research was a necessary (e.g. a significant contributing factor among many) or a sufficient (e.g. sole, direct attribution) cause of impact; and
- The scope of your audience's interest (e.g. some funders are only interested in instrumental impacts, especially economic benefits, which may contrast with your own wider interests).

CHOOSING THE RIGHT EVALUATION METHODS

To decide which methods will most effectively enable you to evaluate your impact, you first need to choose an evaluation design. Think of it like research design. Before you dive into any specific methodology, you first zoom out and think about the most appropriate overall research design. The same holds true for impact evaluation. Therefore, your first task is to choose an appropriate evaluation design. Although this might feel alien to you if you've had no training in evaluation, it is exactly the same process you use as a researcher on a regular basis when designing research projects. Once you realise that evaluation design is simply a type of research design, you are empowered to use your existing skills to evaluate your impact. This can sometimes lead to win-wins where an impact evaluation can be integrated into an existing project or publication, providing stronger research outputs at the same time as providing peer-reviewed evidence of impact. In some cases, however, it will become apparent quite quickly that you and your team do not have the skills necessary to generate the evidence you need. For example, you may have the skills and resources to design a randomised control trial to demonstrate the effectiveness of a new treatment or intervention, but you may need help to do the health economics work necessary to show the cost savings this made to the health service. In these cases, you know the expertise you will need and can start to look for the resources necessary to get the help you need.

Generally speaking, there are five broad types of evaluation design you can choose from, which I describe in the remainder of this section. To help prioritise the most appropriate evaluation design (and hence identify relevant methods within that design), you can use the decision tree in Figure 13.2.

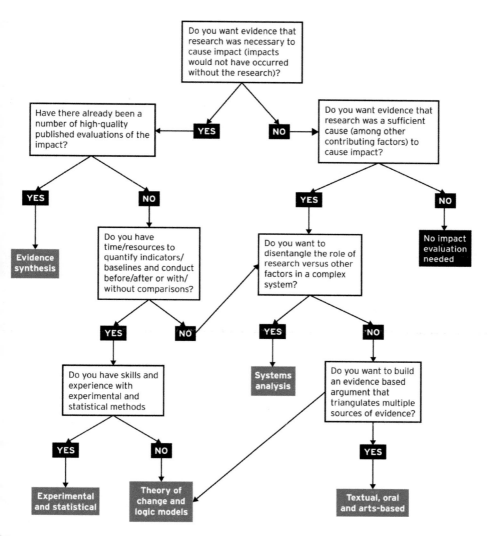

Figure 13.2 Decision tree to select the most appropriate evaluation design, from which methods can then be chosen to evidence policy impacts.

Indicator-based approaches

- **Description**: Indicator-based approaches identify variables that indicate the achievement of impacts. Indicators may be used prospectively during planning as milestones and targets and then retrospectively to see if planned impacts were achieved. Indicators may be identified, organised and evaluated in categories (e.g. economic or environmental benefits) or logical structures (e.g. Logic Models and Theory of Change). Any method may then be used to evaluate each indicator (e.g. economics and interviews are commonly used to evaluate benefits arising from seven stages of the research cycle in the Payback Framework).

- **Methods** include Theory of Change, Logical Framework Analysis, Payback Framework and other Logic Models.
- **Examples** include a change in pre-established indicators set at the start of a project that would be expected to show change as impacts occur, for example number of farm advisors adapting their discourse to farmers, numbers of farmers taking up the conservation measure, hectares of land restored, followed by reduction in water pollution, savings to water companies and reductions in water bills; access to health care, number of individuals getting immunised against a particular disease, number of individuals not contracting the disease followed by reduction in the predominance of the disease and savings in health expenditures; or surveys of target groups showing that understanding is growing and attitudes are changing despite the fact that there is no evidence of a behaviour change yet (attention is then paid to the link between awareness/attitudes and behaviour to see if more time or a new strategy is needed to reach the ultimate change that was proposed in the Theory of Change).

Experimental and statistical

- **Description**: Experimental and statistical methods for impact evaluation typically provide evidence of research as a sufficient cause of impact. This is often done by inferring counterfactual causation, based on the difference between two otherwise identical cases, one that is manipulated and the other that is controlled giving rise to evidence of cause and effect.
- **Methods** include statistical modelling, longitudinal analysis, econometrics, difference-in-difference method, double difference method, propensity score matching, instrumental variables, analysis of distributional effects and experimental economics.
- **Examples**: Randomised control trials or epidemiological studies showing the effectiveness of a policy intervention in a relevant population; improvements in water quality based on improved regulation arising from research; monetary benefits arising from a change in asset

management practices in financial organisations based on new financial services regulation; optimisation in the choice of policy instrument to promote a specific land management technique, informed by research; improvements in indicators of social cohesion or social mobility within a defined perimeter/community; and time, money, ecosystem variables or lives saved as a result of new evidence-based policies.

Textual, oral and arts-based methods

- **Description**: Textual, oral and arts-based evaluation methods tend to build a case that research was necessary to cause impact by triangulating multiple sources of evidence to create a credible, evidence-based argument that attributes impacts to research. All of these methods can be participatory, engaging beneficiaries and other relevant parties in the evaluation itself, enabling these groups to engage and shape the evaluation, which then has the potential to further enhance impact.
- **Methods** include testimonials, ethnography, participant observation, qualitative comparative analysis, linkage and exchange model, interviews and focus groups, opinion polls and surveys, other textual analysis, for example, of focus group and interview data, participatory monitoring and evaluation, empowerment evaluation, action research and associated methods, aesthetics, oral history, storytelling, digital cultural mapping, (social) media analysis, poetry and fiction, music and dance and theatre.
- **Examples**: Testimonials or statements from end users (e.g. policymakers) now applying a modelling tool; testimonials from practitioners explaining how they gained a higher level of capability and capacity handling daily work, thanks to new policy guidance (improved skills, understanding and confidence levels); improvements in variables that indicate the achievement of goals set by an organisation or other social group who co-produced research (e.g. number of community members having acquired a particular skill); changes in culture, cultural discourse or appreciation and benefit from cultural artefacts and experiences.

Systems analysis methods

- **Description**: Systems and pathway analysis methods attempt to disentangle the messy complexity of impacts that occur in complex systems (compared to logic and theory-driven approaches that are used in a more linear way and often also used in impact planning). They tend to draw on a range of qualitative and quantitative research methods to depict more complex cause-and-effect relationships. They are able to capture the complex range of other factors mediating impacts, to enable the generation of arguments that the research made a significant contribution to the impact, even if direct and sole attribution is not possible.

- **Methods** include contribution analysis, knowledge mapping, Social Network Analysis, Bayesian networks, agent-based models, Dynamic System Models, influence diagrams, Participatory Systems Mapping and Bayesian Updating.
- **Example**: A significant contribution made by research to the solution of a previously intractable policy problem, increase and strengthening of the number of nodes or connections in a policy network following a participatory process and understanding of how a group of actors relate to each other and act.

Evidence synthesis approaches

- **Description**: While each of the preceding methods or approaches can be used as part of a project cycle, evidence synthesis typically takes place at the programme level and draws on bodies of work emerging from multiple projects that have sought to evaluate policy outcomes. Evidence synthesis is especially useful where there is apparently contradictory evidence across a range of studies about the relationship between a policy intervention arising from research (e.g. a new piece of regulation, subsidy or guidelines) and impact (e.g. studies reporting positive, negative or no association between the policy and outcomes that are valued as impacts). Evidence synthesis is a process of carrying out a review of existing data, literature and other forms of evidence with predefined methodological approaches, to provide a transparent rigorous and objective assessment of whether something arising from research is a sufficient cause of impactful outcomes. Its use is now widespread across many sectors of society in which research can be used to influence and inform decision-making.
- **Methods** include meta-analysis, narrative synthesis, realist-based synthesis, rapid evidence synthesis and systematic reviews.

- **Example**: Meta-analysis of multiple studies to robustly demonstrate the time, money or lives saved as a result of new evidence-based policies or other evidence of benefits for those affected by the policy.

COMMON APPROACHES TO POLICY IMPACT EVALUATIONS

I will conclude this chapter with some examples of the sorts of methods that are commonly used to evaluate different types of policy impacts, showing how a range of evaluation methods can be integrated in different research designs. I have prioritised popular methods that are well adapted to evaluating policy impacts but that are not too resource intensive.

It is useful to start with an analysis of your pathways to impact or policy engagement. Although this is not impact, collecting evidence of each step you've taken so far in the impact pathway can be useful for identifying opportunities for evaluation. Furthermore, if you plan out your pathways, it may be possible to build in monitoring and evaluation as you go, making your evaluation task much easier. For example, you may have started by responding to a consultation, before adapting your consultation response to create a policy brief, which you may have then taken to a policy seminar and some meetings. Although none of this is impact (yet), and you have no idea what (if anything) happened after your seminar and meetings, you now have a number of clear targets for monitoring (if you plan ahead) and evaluation.

In this example:

- You might look for the government's response to the consultation to see if your response is used or cited or if at least it looks like some of your evidence or ideas have been reflected in the response document;
- You might then look in the response and any documentation around the response for any recommendations or actions that have been proposed and start investigating whether or not these have been actioned;
- You might identify the policy team who were responsible for managing the consultation and the person who led on drawing up the response and seek an interview with them to determine whether or not your evidence shaped the points that appear to relate to your work;
- You might contact people you sent your policy brief to and contact people in policy networks who shared or commented on your policy

brief on social media to ask if they did anything with what they learned from your work; and

- If you presented your policy brief at a seminar, webinar or meeting, you might be able to follow up with participants via the organiser, inviting them to complete an online survey, asking if they have used what they learned in policy or if they have had any challenges that you could help with.

In the remainder of this section, I will review some of these methodological suggestions in greater depth. The majority of these methods fall under the category of textual, oral and arts-based methods, as these are particularly well suited to the evaluation of impacts on policy and policy processes. However, if you have strong evidence that a policy was influenced by your research and you want to seek evidence of public benefits from the implementation of that policy, it may be more effective to look at experimental, statistical, indicator-based and evidence synthesis methods. Systems analysis methods are very effective for evaluating policy impacts but typically take significant amounts of expertise and resources. The methods that follow can be used in both formative and summative mode to provide feedback to enhance your engagement as well as providing evidence of actual impacts. You will not be able to build an argument that your research had impact using any one of these methods in isolation. Instead, you will be seeking to infer causal links between your research and impact by building a case (sometimes jointly with beneficiaries) that triangulates multiple sources of evidence to create an evidence-based, credible argument for research being a necessary cause of impact (among other factors).

Citation analysis

- **Peer-reviewed citations**: Although rare, it is possible to find evidence of policy impacts in the peer-reviewed literature, especially if you have published a particularly influential theory, framework or method which becomes widely used in a range of applied settings. To do this, look for citations in applied journals and different disciplines to your own, then scan titles and abstracts, only looking in depth at the few that look like they may be reporting a policy application of your work. Typically once you have identified such an application, you will need to reach out to the lead author to find out more, either conducting a testimonial interview with them (see below) or asking them to put you in touch with policy colleagues they have worked with so that you can interview individuals who were more directly involved in the policy work.

- **Policy citations**: Again it is rare to find many examples of this, but if there are direct citations to your work in policy documents, this could be important evidence to help attribute impacts to your research. The easiest way to do this is via Altmetric (see above), but it is worth bearing in mind that their database is biased towards English-speaking democracies and international policy organisations. Therefore, you may wish to supplement this with targeted internet searches for countries you think are likely to have drawn on your research. You will typically need to follow up to see what happened to these documents – if they were action plans, strategies or committee reports; were the recommendations ever implemented; and did they contribute towards legislation, binding targets or regulation etc? It may be possible to establish a causal link between multiple documents which, when taken together, despite not leading to an actual policy change yet, may demonstrate significant influence on policy processes. When you start doing testimonial interviews (see Testimonial interview section), you will also want to ask if those you interview are aware of citations to your work that you might not have picked up online, and this can also include documents that were in reality shaped by your research, but that don't cite you.

Social media analysis

This can be an inexpensive way of identifying individuals and organisations that may have benefited from your research so that you can follow up with them via online surveys and/or testimonial interviews (see Survey work and Testimonial interviews sections) to learn more about impacts on organisations you might otherwise not have known had benefited. Social media analysis might sound like a daunting prospect if you have not done it before, but it can be surprisingly accessible:

- Quantitative content analysis can be used to count the frequency with which particular words or phrases appear in media (and trends can be tracked over time, looking for peaks that might correspond to policy engagement activities). Similarly, this technique can be used to characterise a body of text that is known to relate to the policy engagement that is being evaluated (e.g. tweets on an event hashtag), based on the frequency of words within that body of text.

- Although more time-consuming, qualitative analysis of text that has been aggregated using a hashtag or keyword search can offer more nuanced insights into the nature of debate stimulated by policy engagement. Changes in the amount and nature of discourse may be tracked over time.
- Evidence of reach may be gathered for particular messages (e.g. number of retweets for particular tweets, and where possible the reach and impressions for that tweet), to evaluate which messages gained most traction.
- It may also be possible to study the diversity of people discussing (or liking or retweeting etc) stories linked to research, or discussing the research directly, where profile information is available, for example based on gender and interests.
- Alternatively, more nuanced findings can be gained from a qualitative analysis of social media comments, identifying key themes and using these to build rich descriptions of different responses to the research illustrated by quotes.
- Finally, it is possible to reach out directly to social media users who made comments to ask additional questions, collecting further qualitative data on the platform or inviting them to take an online survey or participate in a telephone interview.
- It is important to note that social media analysis comes with a number of limitations and ethical challenges. Social media users are unlikely to be representative of the overall audience engaging with the media, for example different platforms have distinct demographic or geographical biases. It is also important to get ethics permission for this sort of evaluation, and different universities often have quite different norms and rules around social media research. While some argue that those posting social media comments understand that the material is available for anyone to view publicly, it is very difficult to prove that you have obtained informed consent from those who posted the comments to analyse them.

Survey work

- **Exit surveys:** It is good to get into the habit of asking people to complete surveys at the end of any policy event you run. Make sure to ask people to reflect on what they would like to do practically with what they have learned during your event, as there is evidence that writing down an intention increases the likelihood that a person follows through on that intention. Also make sure that you ask permission to follow up with people after the event (GDPR compliant), as impacts tend to mature over time, as people act on what they learned and benefits start to accrue. To encourage people to give their permission for this, you might also ask participants to think about potential barriers that might prevent them from achieving their intention, and say that if they give you permission, you will follow up with them personally after a set period of time (ideally one to three months after the event) to find out how they are getting on and offer them help as necessary to follow through with their intention. The 'postcard to your future self' is a type of exit survey, although you only get to ask one question alongside your request to be granted permission to follow them up. It has the advantage of being quick and easy for people to complete, and in addition to following up with those who gave you permission, you send the postcards back to people by post after a set period of time. As a result, those who are not followed up by you receive a message from themselves by post, reminding them of the intention they formed (Figure 13.3).
- **Online surveys** are a good way of getting a large amount of data quickly, but response rates can be low and it is easy to build in biases to your data inadvertently. Online surveys are useful when you're not sure who might have used your research. For example, I knew that our research had influenced international policy resolutions on the basis of a testimonial interview (see Testimonial interviews section below). However, I had no idea which of the hundreds of countries around the world with peatlands might have implemented the resolution, as countries were not mandated to report whether or not they had developed peatland policies in response to the resolution. As a result, our team launched an online survey, which we sent in three different languages to every country that contained peatlands. As the response rate was very low, more intensive follow-up calls were made to the countries with the peatlands that were producing

How might you use what you learned today into policy or practise (or what you need to use what you learned)?

Tick this box for a researcher to contact you to see if you need help putting what you learned today into practise, and to receive electronic copies of the policy briefs and presentations. We will not use your e-mail for any other purpose or pass it to any third parties. Contact data will be stored securely by Newcastle University and will be GDPR compliant.

Email address:

Figure 13.3 Example of 'a postcard to your future self' used in a policy seminar.

the highest greenhouse gas emissions. This resulted in evidence o new peatland policies, in response to the resolution, in 29 countries Similarly, you might suspect that a particular agency has used you research but have no idea which team to approach. In this case, yo would target your survey to employees of the agency via interna mailing lists where you have a warm contact in the organisation or vi a targeted LinkedIn search, adding employees of the agency to you professional network before sending them each a link to your surve via LinkedIn mail. Online surveys are also useful when you have a ver well defined but large population of potential beneficiaries, for exampl people who have attended a series of training sessions designed t build capacity within policy networks. If you have trained thousand of people, even a low response rate should give you a flavour of th range of benefits people have gained since attending the training. I you then include a question asking if you can follow them up with a interview, you can then target individuals with particularly significan or interesting impacts, to explore these in greater depth.

- **Large-scale interviewing and focus groups**: Although time-consuming and expensive, qualitative analysis of in-depth interviews (not to be confused with structured questionnaires), combined with focus groups, can provide rich data on impacts that would be too difficult for people to express explicitly in response to a survey. However, through discussion in an interview or focus group setting, they may be able to articulate a range of impacts that you might otherwise miss. This approach is particularly useful if you are trying to build capacity within a policy organisation and change understanding or attitudes among a group of policy colleagues or if you are seeking broader cultural change in the way an organisation or group operates. However, in most cases, your task is to find a much smaller group of individuals who have actually been responsible for designing policy mechanisms and drafting policy documents, who can talk very specifically about the contribution your research made to a policy. To do this, you will most likely opt for a small number of testimonial interviews instead.

Testimonial interviews

- Testimonial interviews are no different to any other in-depth interview. The only difference is that you are targeting a small number of people who you believe are likely to be able to provide you with evidence about the impact of your work (in social science, this would be called a purposive sample of key informant interviews). Conduct testimonial interviews face-to-face if possible, or by phone or video call. Explain that the interview will consist of two parts: first getting an understanding of each other's current work and seeing if there's any way you can help them further, and then moving on to ask questions about the impact of your previous work with them.
- Get research ethics permission and informed consent to do your interviews, as you will be recording and transcribing them, and most policy colleagues will want know what you will do with the recordings and transcripts before they are willing to talk on the record.
- Contact key people you think may be able to tell you about impacts from your work, inviting them to interview and asking them to complete your consent form.
- Use the first half of your interview for a catch-up and updates, and the second half for the interview (for people you are regularly in touch

with, you can skip straight to the second half and organise a 30-minute interview). Consider sending a plain English summary of some of your latest research or bringing it along with you if meeting face-to-face.

- Before the interview segment, make sure you get informed consent to record, explaining what will happen with the recording, giving them a countersigned copy of the consent form and keeping a copy yourself. Make sure you and they are clear about whether they are providing a personal testimony or one on behalf of their organisation (typically the latter as you will want to be able to quote their position in the organisation to underscore the legitimacy of what they have said about your research).

- During the interview segment, ask four questions: i) have there been any significant benefits arising from your research? ii) how far-reaching are those benefits? iii) to what extent can these benefits be attributed to your research versus other factors? and iv) did anything negative happen as a result of your research? If the answer to the first question is that there have been no significant benefits, then skip the next two questions and check if anything negative happened as a result of your work. This last question is important as a robust research impact evaluation should always aim to consider both positive and negative impacts, in case there is anything you can do to mitigate things that went wrong or learn for future practice. You don't need to be a social scientist or an experienced interviewer to do this. You just need to understand the concepts of significance, reach and attribution and so be able to recognise if a person has given you an answer that tells you an impact is significant, far-reaching and linked to your research. If the answer doesn't do this, then you keep probing until you are clear that there is genuinely nothing of significance to report.

- Where possible, ask for evidence to support the claims they are making, collecting documents or names of other people to follow up with.

- Get your recording transcribed, and highlight the sections that are most relevant.

- Email the highlighted transcript to your interviewee, asking them to write a letter (on their organisation's headed paper) outlining the main points from the interview, based on the highlighted sections. The transcript should make it significantly quicker and easier for them to do this.

- You may want to get a concise, quotable summary of the key points made in the testimony, which you can quote in a case study without using up too much space. You can ask for this, or you can propose your own summary based on their testimonial and ask them to amend it, so they are happy with it, for inclusion in their letter.

I was glad that I followed this approach when I found myself in an acutely embarrassing testimonial interview with someone who had mistaken me for someone else. I had followed Dianna Kopansky from the United Nation (UN) Environment Programme to the international climate summit in Poland after introducing myself to her and learning that she was already using my work. I started by finding out more about the Global Peatlands Initiative she was leading, to find points of common interest, where I might be able to help her. We then moved to the testimonial interview and I got out my voice recording app and consent form. But within minutes, it became apparent that the research she was familiar with wasn't my research. I hurriedly turned off the voice recorder and put away the consent form, pivoting back to our original conversation, to try and identify some actions we could follow up on. Within two years, I had found funding to lead a major piece of work for her initiative on standardising how data was collected so we could better synthesise evidence for peatland policy. This led to an opportunity to become a lead author on a global synthesis report, helping her co-author the summary for policymakers. I helped her and others create the first ever pavilion dedicated to peatland policy at the climate summit in Glasgow, which helped spawn the European Peatlands Initiative. And I am now working with her to gather evidence gaps from peatland policy teams internationally, while training researchers in evidence synthesis to fill those gaps, in my role as co-chair of the Global Peatlands Initiative Research Working Group. All of these activities were captured in a subsequent testimonial interview two years later, in which I felt significantly less embarrassed than I did in our first meeting.

COLLABORATIVE EVALUATIONS

Finally, it is worth pointing out that your colleagues from policy and third-sector organisations are also likely to need evidence of impact, and you may be able to join forces with them. Not only might this enable you to spread the evaluation workload; you can also share the outcomes and further help your colleagues. In the policy world, there is an extensive policy appraisal process to ensure proposed changes in policy, regulation and spending are beneficial (or benign) in environmental, social and economic terms. These often include detailed strategic, environmental and social impact assessments, cost-benefit analyses and other economic assessments and the use of experiments and quasi-experimental impact evaluation methods. For example, the UK government provides guidance from its Green Book (for appraisal of proposed policies) and Magenta Book (for evaluation of existing and previous policies). As a researcher, it is possible to: 1) advise on the design of appraisals, monitoring programmes and evaluations; 2) be contracted to carry out appraisals and evaluations as a consultant; and 3) propose that a policy is evaluated, especially if it is coming up to an important milestone and you think there is evidence that the policy might not be working as planned. Although the teams you contact are under no obligation to carry out the evaluation you have suggested, and probably don't have time to do this themselves, if you offer to help, you may increase the likelihood of an evaluation being carried out.

Before I finish this chapter, it is worth considering how you will write up the evidence you have collected. In an ideal world, depending on your discipline, it may be possible to write up your evaluation as a peer reviewed article in its own right (for an example of this, see Reed et al. 2018, in Further Reading). If this is not possible, then consider whether your impact evaluation might contribute to ongoing research, for example as a section of paper or an epilogue to a monograph. Alternatively, you could write up your evaluation informally as a blog or project report or offer it as a contribution to a trade magazine, newsletter or annual report via your policy networks.

Evaluating, evidencing and celebrating policy impacts might be a good place to end a book on influencing policy. It is certainly an important end point that you should have in mind when you are planning and carrying out your policy engagement work. But as you finish this book, I want you to return to the deeper, longer term work of interrogating your values and privilege and transforming yourself so that you can play a more transformative role in policy.

CHAPTER 14

Conclusion and further reading

The worlds of research and policy are so different that many researchers experience culture shock when they first start working between the two worlds. If you are experiencing this now, having reached the end of this book, then you are faced with two options. First, you could disengage and go no further. If you are just starting your career and feel that engaging in policy work now requires more time and courage than you currently possess, it is rational to prioritize your research. Gradually build your confidence and policy networks, preparing for meaningful engagement in the future, rather than seeking quick wins that may be unsustainable and offer limited benefits to policy partners or society.

Your second option is to start engaging or continuing to engage in new ways, based on what you have learned in this book. You will do so with more realistic expectations than you might have had when you started the book. You now understand how complex and unpredictable policy systems are and your policy colleagues often have no more power than you do to make the changes you each want to see. You realise that there is no such thing as a policymaker but rather multiple policy teams in government departments, agencies and other bodies, serving politicians, who are part of a wider network of organisations outside government that move in and out of influence as their agendas overlap with the programme of government. You are not just trying to win friends and influence people in high places, but you are aware of your power to listen to and represent the perspectives of those whose voices are rarely heard in the corridors of power, alongside the evidence from your research. You are aware of how your personal values and beliefs shape your research interests and influence your perception of policy problems

DOI: 10.4324/9781003494942-17

and the most appropriate ways of tackling them. As a result, you know that there will be setbacks, and things are unlikely to go according to plan. But if you remain sufficiently curious and open and are humble enough to learn from own your mistakes as much as you learn from your policy colleagues, then you might be able to empathise with your policy colleagues and the many pressures and constraints they are under. It is this empathic connection that is the foundation for friendship and trust. Trust is why people will keep coming back to you for help. Trust is why you will stay with your policy colleagues through the ups and downs of policy development, all the way through to the implementation of the policies you helped shape. Because you now see the importance of evaluation you will collect evidence as you go, helping undo the policies that don't actually work in the real world and building on what does work, to make the world an even better place.

It is not a perfect system; in fact, it is not a system at all, in any planned sense of the word. But the complexity of challenges that public policies around the world are trying to address requires new ideas and curious minds like yours. They also need a diversity of people, perspectives and approaches, and in some cases, rather than centring our own expertise our task is to get out of the way so that the expertise of others, whose knowledge and perspectives are often undervalued and ignored, can find their rightful place alongside the research evidence that tends to dominate policy advice.

To do this effectively, you will need to do more than just read a book, though. This is deep work, and it will take many of us years before we see meaningful progress. Our most problematic beliefs and assumptions are often hidden from our view, and they can pervade all aspects of our lives, if we do not become aware of them and start to tackle the values and attitudes that lie beneath them. It has taken me years to recognise the epistemic racism of my PhD research which used Western scientific methods to 'validate' the local knowledge of Kalahari pastoralists. It took even longer to recognise the 'everyday sexism' of my dismissal of risks that only my wife can perceive. I struggle to this day to overcome the structural barriers that make it so difficult for research colleagues in teaching intensive institutions in the Global South to engage in policy relevant research as equal partners.

This is work in progress, and it is difficult, painful work recognising your flaws, failings, biases and prejudices. But it is the only work that matters if we are to go beyond saying the right things to really changing how we act. If we could take our eyes for a moment from our aspirations for national and international policy impacts and do this inner work, our friends, family and colleagues will be the first people to benefit from our journey towards policy impact. Only once we have got our own house in order, can we start to build policy relationships that will last and policy impacts that will benefit the least privileged in society. It is time to get out of the echo chamber or research and policy elites and to start getting our hands dirty with the messy reality of real-world policy work.

FURTHER READING

Cairney, P., 2019. *Understanding public policy.* 2nd Edition. Red Globe Press.

Cairney, P., 2021. *The politics of policy analysis.* Palgrave Macmillan.

Cairney, P., Heikkila, T. and Wood, M., 2019. *Making policy in a complex world.* Cambridge University Press.

Carrigan, M., 2019. *Social media for academics.* Sage.

Hall, G., Morley, H. and Bromley, T., 2019. Uncertainty and Confusion: The Starting Point of All Expertise. In: Fenby-Hulse, K., Heywood, E. and Walker, K., eds., *Research impact and the early career researcher lived experiences.* Routledge.

Khuri, S. and Reed, M.S., 2020. *Tips and tools for making your online meetings and workshops more interactive.* Fast Track Impact. Available online at: https://www.fasttrackimpact. com/post/tips-and-tools-for-making-your-online-meetings-and-workshops-more-interactive.

Morgan, K., Steenmans, I., Tennant, G. and Green, R., 2022. *Engaging with evidence toolkit. A practical resource to strengthen capabilities for evidence use and expert engagement.* Nesta.

Oliver, K. and Cairney, P., 2019. The dos and don'ts of influencing policy: a systematic review of advice to academics. *Palgrave Communications* 5(1): 1–11.

Pielke Jr, R.A., 2007. *The honest broker: making sense of science in policy and politics.* Cambridge University Press.

Reed, M.S., 2018. *The research impact handbook.* 2nd edition, Fast Track Impact.

Reed, M.S. and Barbrook-Simpson, P., 2022. Complex systems methods for impact evaluation: lessons from the evaluation of an environmental boundary organisation. *Mires & Peat* 34:1–14.

Reed, M.S., Bryce, R. and Machen, R., 2018. Pathways to policy impact: a new approach for planning and evidencing research impact. *Evidence & Policy* 14:431–458.

Reed, M.S., Ferre, M., Martin-Ortega, J., Blanche, R., Dallimer, M., Lawford-Rolfe, R. and Holden, J., 2021. Evaluating research impact: a methodological framework. *Research Policy* 50:104–147.

Reed, M.S., Jensen, J.A., Kendall, H., Noles, S., Raley, M., Tarrant, A., Oakley, N., Hinson, C. and Hoare, V., under review. Analyzing who is relevant to engage in decision-making processes by interests, influence and impact: the 3i methodological framework. *Journal of Environmental Management.*

Reichard, B., Reed, M.S., Chubb, J., Hall, G., Jowett, L., Paert, A., 2020. Writing Impact Case Studies: A comparative study of high-scoring and low-scoring case studies from REF 2014. *Palgrave Communications* 6: 31.

Tricco, A.C., Langlois, E., Straus, S.E. and World Health Organization, 2017. *Rapid reviews to strengthen health policy and systems: a practical guide.* World Health Organization.

UK Parliament. 2021. *Research impact at the UK Parliament: everything you need to know to engage with Parliament as a researcher.* HMSO.

Vorley, T., Abdul Rahman, S., Tuckerman, L. and Wallace, P., eds., 2022. *How to engage policy makers with your research: the art of informing and impacting policy.* Edward Elgar Publishing.

Index

decolonising research for policy impact 73–77
Development in Practice (Rowlands) 75
de Vente, Joris 78
double-loop learning 66
doughnut model 153, *153*
Dunn, Helen 29, 31
Dunning, David 32
Dunning-Kruger effect 32, *33*

E
early career researcher (ECR) 8, 29–31, 34, 51, 86, 109, *154*, 155
ecological dynamics model 37
Ecology & Society 78
economic growth 36
education policy 5
electronic communication 63
empathic connection 34, 61, 196
empathy 8, 28, 39, 78, 91; bias 61; skills 65
English government 38, 64, 72
environmental destruction 36
epistemology 114, 118, 139, 179
Europe's 8th Environment Action Programme 153
Evidence and Policy (Bandola) 68
evidence-based interventions 105
evidence-based policy 1, 7–8, 22–24, 68
evidence-informed policy 22
evidence synthesis 5, 14, 85–87, 90, 105, 155, 170, 193; approaches 184–185; element of 141–142; example of *128–128*; and policy brief 125–130; rapid 127; Theory of Change 93
exit surveys 189
expert: broker 115, 116; collaborator 116; influencer 110; informer 110

F
facilitating broker 116
facilitating collaborator 116, 138
facilitating influencer 111, 138
facilitating informer 110
factors influencing policy decisions 24
Few, Roger 78
Forrester, Jay 36
Fraire, Josie Valadez 47
Freeman, Edward 47

G
General Data Protection Regulation (GDPR) 161
genetically modified (GM) crops 21
Geo: Geography and Environment (Sultana) 79

Geographical Journal 78
Global Environmental Change 78
goal hierarchy theory 34
Golden Plover 79
government-funded research 51
Green, Duncan 102
green paper 124
green revolution policies 21
The Guardian 164

H
Haldane, Richard 114
Haldane principle 114
Hall, Peter 39
Hamper, Josie *137*
Harris, Eleanor 104
healthcare systems 17
Hen Harriers 79
high-integrity ecosystem markets *54*
Hong Kong's Research Assessment Exercise 22
How Change Happens (Green) 102
How to Engage Policymakers with Your Research: The Art of Informing and Impacting Policy (Vorley) 23
How to Win Campaigns: Communications for Change (Rose) 164
human behaviour 37, 130
humility 8, 28, 60
Huntly Development Trust 79

I
impact culture 25
Impact Culture (Reed) 31
impact guru 33
imposter syndrome 29–34
industrialise agriculture 21
influence/influencing policy 1–2, 14, 163–174; commissioned research 172–174; factors 24; policy fellowships, shadowing and internships 169–171; policy sprints 171–172; responding to policy consultations 168–169; testifying to inquiries and committees 167–168; via social and mass media 163–166
influencing mode of policy engagement 110
informing mode of policy engagement 110
interest, influence and impact **48**, 48–51, **49–50**
Intergovernmental Panel on Climate Change 111

J
Journal of Personality and Social Psychology 32
Journal of Social Policy 5